"The essays are heartfelt, surprising, and show there's no one path to becoming a writer. . . . Aspiring poets will find a rich vein of insight in these thoughtful pieces."

PUBLISHERS WEEKLY

———

"*On Becoming a Poet* gratifyingly is not a how-to for becoming one. These are the stories of what transpired as and when the realization occurred. Or: 'The first time it happened,' to use Mary Mackey's phrase. 'It'—the proximate cause, and then the poetry itself—was a pepperwood tree. It was a Mrs. Sullivan who stopped to care. It was the nomination of Robert Bork. It was the school chorus as an opt-out from gym. It was a translation of a Tang dynasty poem into English. Find these instigations here and then find yours."

AL FILREIS
Kelly Writers House, University of Pennsylvania

———

"*On Becoming a Poet* is a necessary text for any active and engaged reader. Whether you're a practicing poet, a teacher looking for more sources, or a lay reader who is just interested in poetry, you'll find something in this text for you. The scale of this text alone makes it worth readers' while: 25 poets from diverse backgrounds revealing their meaning-making strategies and poetry origins stories! The personal component of this text is so compelling and helps the text to teach without being overly didactic. This book is a blessing and needed addition to the archive and canon."

DOUGLAS MANUEL
Bayard Rustin Fellow, Whittier College

———

"Here in abundant variety are clear insights on the life of art. This brilliar readers and writers alike, to anyon(

**BRENDAN CONSTⱯ

D0488018

On Becoming a Poet

Becoming a Poet

25 ORIGINAL ESSAYS + INTERVIEWS

EDITED BY SUSAN TERRIS

SERIES EDITOR: SANDY McINTOSH

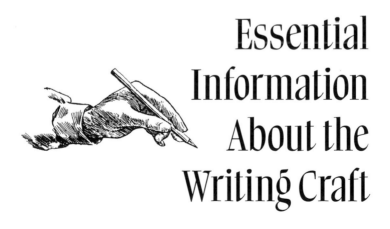

Essential Information About the Writing Craft

Marsh Hawk Press · 2022

EAST ROCKAWAY, NEW YORK

Marsh Hawk books are published by Marsh Hawk Press, Inc.,
a not-for-profit corporation under section 501(c)3
United States Internal Revenue Code.

Book design & typesetting: Mark Melnick
Page 11: photograph of Kim Shuck by Douglas A. Salin
Page 87: photograph of Geoffrey O'Brien by Nina Subin

FIRST EDITION

Library of Congress Cataloging-in-Publication Data
Names: Terris, Susan, editor.
Title: On becoming a poet / edited by Susan Terris.
Description: First edition. | East Rockaway : Marsh Hawk Press, 2022. |
Includes bibliographical references.
Identifiers: LCCN 2021062847 | ISBN 9781732614130 (paperback)
Subjects: LCSH: Poets, American--20th century--Biography. | Poets,
American--21st century--Biography. | Creation (Literary, artistic, etc.)
| Poetry--Authorship. | LCGFT: Interviews. | Essays. | Autobiographies.
Classification: LCC PS135 .O6 2022 | DDC 811/.609--dc23/eng/20220124
LC record available at https://lccn.loc.gov/2021062847

Publication of this title was made possible in part by a regrant awarded
and administered by the Community of Literary Magazines and Presses (CLMP).
CLMP's NYS regrant programs are made possible by the New York State Council on
the Arts with the support of Governor Kathy Hochul and the New York State Legislature.

Marsh Hawk Press
P.O. Box 206, East Rockaway, N.Y. 11518-0206
mheditor@marshhawkpress.org

Introduction

THIS ANTHOLOGY FEATURES THE ORIGINAL MEMOIRS of outstanding poets from diverse backgrounds, recalling the ways by which they found their start as writers. It includes twenty-five original essays and interviews appearing here in print for the first time. While modern creative writing programs seek to develop the talents of maturing writers, essential information about the initiation, development and processes of the writing craft can be discovered in the early memories of established writers—material that has not usually been available in the classroom.

Reading the essays and interviews in this anthology, you'll discover:

· How poets find their voices

· How they perfect their craft

· How they deal with racial and gender discrimination

· How, despite rejection and disappointment, they keep on writing

· Why many poets will need a Plan B to support themselves outside academia

· Why high fevers and near death-experiences inspired one poet

· Why another's success prompted him to apologize to his high school English teacher

· Why two poets began to write inspired by story-telling fathers.

· Which poet believed a pepperwood tree taught her how to write

· You will meet a poet who focuses on the door inside her head

· A poet who created and illustrated her first book when she was five

· A poet inspired to write because of an alleged UFO invasion

· And much more . . .

These amusing, compelling and inspiring memoirs return to the ideas and visions the contributors found as young poets, and the experiences that have defined the path for their writing over a lifetime. There are, of course, far more than twenty-five ways to become a poet, but these are some of the most compelling.

Sandy McIntosh

Series Editor | Publisher, Marsh Hawk Press, Inc.

———

Online Resources for Students, Instructors and Readers are available at

chapter-one.marshhawkpress.org

Writing Prompts & Insights | Poetic Influences | Poet's Biographies | Videos

Contents

Mary Mackey

Indigo Moor

Kim Shuck

Philip F. Clark

Gail Newman

Basil King

Mary Mackey

Fever and Jungles: On Becoming a Poet

I DO NOT HAVE AN MFA. I became a poet by running high fevers, tramping through tropical jungles, dodging machine gun fire, and being caught in volcanic eruptions, swarmed by army ants, stalked by vampire bats, threatened by poisonous snakes, and making catastrophic decisions with regard to men. And then there was reading.

I read constantly, compulsively: secretly under the covers with a flashlight after I had been put to bed; defiantly when I was supposed to be doing the dishes or sweeping the kitchen; sneakily in any class that was boring. As proof that my reading addiction was out of hand, I offer the fact that I was quite possibly the only student at North Central High School ever to be sent to the principle for being in illicit possession of a collection of the poems of William Blake. (Fortunately, when she busted me, my math teacher did not find Ovid's highly erotic *The Art of Love*, which had somehow made it into our school library uncensored.)

How did Jungle Woman and Bookworm come to inhabit the same body? How did they combine to make a little girl born in Indianapolis, Indiana, during the height of McCarthyism into a short, scrappy woman who began writing poems at the age of eleven and never stopped? The answer is both simple and complex.

The simple part is that I desperately wanted to get out of Indianapolis. About the time I turned eleven, I started to realize that everything interesting was happening somewhere else. I had even heard rumors that in Paris people sat around in things called "cafes" and talked about ideas.

Paris, Rome, Antarctica, Mars: how, despite an impaired sense of geography, I longed to see them firsthand. Books had already taken me to exotic places—OZ among them—but I had never really been anywhere unless you counted trips to the family farm in Kentucky and a brief jaunt to Niagara Falls where I got to enter a foreign country for the first time, albeit not a very exotic-looking one.

I imagine many of the children I went to school with also longed to go somewhere interesting, but I had an advantage. I knew that there were places so different from Indianapolis that they could not be described in ordinary words; and this is where it gets complex, because the thing that brought me this knowledge, the thing that did more than anything else to make me into a poet, was fever. But first it almost killed me.

The first time it happened, I was six months old. I don't remember any of the events of my near-death experience, but I'm told I turned blue and went into convulsions. According to my mother, I would have died except that my father, who was completing his medical training in a military hospital, had access to penicillin—a drug not at the time available to civilians. The stuff was nasty: preserved in wax in a small glass bottle that had to be boiled before the penicillin was injected via a very large, hollow needle.

For most of my childhood, I dreaded that wax and that huge needle so much that I had to be chased and pinned down like a cat being taken to the vet, but on the night I nearly died before I had lived, the penicillin bought down my fever and saved my life. But fever was not done with me.

The next time I nearly died was just before my third birthday. I remember that experience well, because it was the first time I saw how thin and bright the world could be. I remember lying on a green couch in a overheated room. It must have been winter because frost coated the window panes, and snow lay on the bare branches of the trees in big lumps. My mother had given me a bottle of Coca-Cola on the principle that I needed to take in more fluids. My temperature must have been somewhere between 105° and 106° Fahrenheit, because I was already experiencing that wonderful, detached, floating feeling I always get above 105°.

Just for the record, the path from 98.6° to 105° is nasty: filled with aches, pains, uncontrolled shaking and the pure misery of sickness, but once you reach 105° everything changes. You start to feel irrationally happy. Your body becomes light and buoyant. By the time you get to 106°, you begin to discover that you are incapable of worrying, even though everyone around you is frantic with fear. The best is yet to come. Teetering on the edge of 107° brings the real poetic gifts, because a fever that high does something strange to your brain.

As I lay on that green couch, warm golden light—the kind you only see for a few moments at sunset—flooded our living room. My parents moved toward me so slowly that I could see their clothing billow out and collapse in an invisible wind. Bending over me, they lost their faces, and floated toward the ceiling like huge birds. The coke bottle on the coffee table multiplied into dozens of coke bottles, which flew up and circled in a huge glassy aura around their heads.

Behind my parents' bodies, the light turned into a veil composed of long, rainbow-colored ribbons. The veil expanded, consuming the green couch, the blankets, the windows, and my parents. Suddenly it parted, and I saw trees with red and gold leaves (impossible, because it was the dead of winter), and little children stretching out their hands and calling to me.

I couldn't have had much of a vocabulary at that age. Nevertheless, words suddenly streamed into my mind and came out of my mouth, combining and recombining into entirely new things. I believe this was the moment I was given the gift of poetry, a gift which I did not yet have the skill or understanding to use, but a gift nevertheless.

I have captured this childhood experience best in a poem entitled *Breaking the Fever* in my collection by the same name (*Breaking the Fever*, Marsh Hawk Press 2011). Although fever is far from the only topic of my poetry, it has provided the specific inspiration for well over a dozen poems and subtle inspiration for many more, many of which are in my most recent collection *The Jaguars That Prowl Our Dreams: New and Selected Poems 1974 to 2018* (Marsh Hawk Press, 2018).

What does fever show me? Are the things I see real? Your guess is as good as mine. I don't claim to be a profit or an oracle. All I know for certain is that something strange happened to me on that afternoon just before my third birthday, something that would happen again at least half a dozen times as I continued to run extraordinarily high fevers. The logical explanation is that I was hallucinating. Yet hallucination does little to explain how well-organized the words I babbled were, and how I sensed them as objects that regrouped and changed forms. Nor does it explain why, much later in life during high fevers, I spoke in rhymed couplets—sometimes for several hours at a time—and was unable to stop until my temperature dipped below 106°.

Actually, I am less interested in discovering an explanation for why these things happen to me than in the result, for starting at a very young age, fever gave me priceless poetic gifts: metaphor, because it showed me how one thing could easily become another; rhythm, because it organized the speech centers of my brain; a love of words, stories, and ideas, which had a life of their own and frequently came into my head so effort-lessly that writing them down was like taking dictation. Best of all, fever gave me chance to see the world in a way that few other people see it. Am I insane? Fair question, but if you are searching for a mad poet, I'm afraid you're in for a disappointment. When I am well and fever-free, which is 99% of the time, I am almost boringly sane. I'm a practical, well-orga-nized, Professor of English, dedicated to poetry as a craft, meticulous about revision, and unless my body temperature goes above 106°, I never hallucinate or speak in rhymed couplets.

Thus, although I received some of the building blocks for creating poems a little before my third birthday, it would be years before I knew what a poem was and many more years before I attempted to write one. Oddly enough, the break-through came in a geometry class. I was eleven, and it was late October. We were learning about triangles, and I was bored in a way that makes you willing to give in to any kind of distraction including counting the tiles in the ceiling. My classroom lacked ceiling tiles, but it did have large windows, which looked out on the front lawn of the school. The leaves had turned on the maples about a week ago, and now the wind was blowing them all over the place, sucking them into the air, whirling them around, and throwing them to the ground.

Up in front of the class, my geometry teacher was talking about obtuse and congruent triangles. *Obtuse. Congruent. What wonderful words,* I thought. At that moment it all came together: the wind, the leaves, the tri-angles, and the geometry lesson. Suddenly, I saw the leaves both as dead leaves and at the same time, as masses of colored light swarming in pat-terns. Suddenly I understood that leaves too could be obtuse and congru-ent. Picking up my pen, I quickly scribbled down my first poem:

> Blown high on the wind unfurled
> Gathered in masses of light
> Softly though their numbered twirls
> The autumn leaves in flight
>
> Reds and yellows, pastels soft
> Shapes obtuse and congruent
> Blown high by the wind aloft
> Motions precise yet fluent

Not a very good poem, admittedly, but very important to me, because it marks the moment I fell forever in love with science, which I suddenly realized was not so different from poetry. Weren't poets and scientists both trying to explain the world around us? Weren't they both exploring the unknown and attempting to make sense of it, trying to figure out how human beings fit in? The vocabulary of science was simply another kind of poetic language, and the beautiful logic of scientific proofs, like the words of a poem, had the same goal: creating meaning out of chaos.

In the weeks that followed, I wrote twenty poems, which flowed out of me so fast I could hardly get them down on paper. In retrospect, none of them were very good, but I loved writing. I was intoxicated with it. I still had no desire to become a poet, have a career in poetry, or get published. I was just having the best kind of fun you can have.

Soon I realized that I had two problems. First, I had no idea what I was doing; and worse yet, I had no control over my poems and no idea how to fix them when they went wrong. Being a practical sort, I decided to read as much poetry as possible, pick it apart, and see how it was put together. I thought I could learn everything I needed to know in a few months, but, of course, I was wrong. Learning my craft took years.

My second problem was that no matter how pretty my poems were or how cleverly I combined words, I didn't have anything significant to write about. I was a child. I was living in Indianapolis. I needed a subject. You might say I needed a life. I couldn't go on talking about autumn leaves forever.

If you don't have a life, I asked myself, *what do you do?* The answer seemed obvious: You borrow one. With this in mind, I plunged into the biographies of poets and novelists, determined to discover how their lives had inspired their work. Soon, I discovered two things: First, the great poets and writers of the world did not for the most part live in Indianapolis; second, they were almost all men.

Male writers, it seemed, could do anything. They could drink themselves silly on absinthe and not give a damn if it rotted their brains. They could have wild affairs with their own sisters, "ladies of the night" (whatever that meant) and other men. They could write passionate poems to their poet lovers; then shoot them down in seedy hotels, do prison time for the crime, and still be worshiped as the gods of poetry. While women poets sat home and knitted, male poets could sign on to whaling ships, meet psychotic sea captains and tattooed harpooners, go to war, and write poems about the tragic slaughter of young men in ways that brought tears to your eyes.

The cards were stacked. Men had the whole world to write about, while I was destined to get a decent education, marry a nice man who would provide for me and my three children, and spend what little free time I could spare from taking wax off the kitchen floor writing poetry on domestic topics. Was there an alternative? I had never read or even seen a poem by Sappho, Elizabeth Bishop, Anna Akhmatova, or Sylvia Plath; and Emily Dickenson had been presented to us by our teachers as a talented, but disturbed, recluse, which didn't make her much of a model.

I didn't want to be a man, but like a man, I wanted to be able to do anything and have the whole world as my subject. Most of all, I wanted to have time to write. Clearly I was going to have to figure out how to support myself in a way that left time for travel and writing.

I never for a moment considered that I could do this by becoming a professional poet. Everyone knew that real poets starved in garrets. All you had to do to figure out that writing poetry was not a viable career path was read François Villon's poem "The Legacy" in which Villon, the best-known French poet of the Late Middle Ages, said he couldn't finish writing a poem because his candle had blown out, he had no fire, and his ink had frozen.

It took me about four years to figure out a plan that seemed to have at least some chance of allowing me eat regularly while giving me time to write and see the world: I decided to get a Ph.D. and teach at the college level. This decision to provide for myself is an essential part of the story of how I became a poet, and it had unexpected benefits.

During all those years of study, I only took one creative writing class, primarily because it was the only one Harvard offered. It was taught by the talented Steven Sandy who gave me the first and only feedback I ever received from a published poet while I was a student. (An interesting sidelight is that to get into Harvard's sole creative writing class, you had to compete against other students by submitting a sample of your work. That year I was the only woman admitted.)

As I sat in Mr. Sandy's creative writing seminar, surrounded by nineteen young men, I was almost a poet, but not yet the poet I wanted to become. I had no mentors: no male poets to take me under their wing, and certainly no female ones because there weren't any at Harvard. I was

still on my own, and the world I was living in—while far more interesting than Indianapolis—was too safe, too predictable, too academic, and
much too rational. I didn't want to write predictable, academic, rational
poetry. I wanted to write poems that explored the world I saw above 106°
without having to deal with starvation, incarceration, and frozen ink.

Fate cooperated. In the fall semester of my senior year, I sat down to
dinner next to a Harvard professor named Richard Evans Schultes. Since
I was an English major, I had no idea who he was or what he had done,
but we had a pleasant conversation about Charles Dickens, whose novel
Pickwick Papers was the subject of my senior honors thesis. It turned out
that Professor Schultes was a member of the Boston chapter of the Dickens Society, and he invited me to come to the Old North Church to cele-
brate Dickens' 153rd birthday.

At this point, you may be asking yourself what this chance encounter had to do with how I became a poet, and my reply is "everything."
After the birthday party, which involved singing "Happy Birthday" to Mr.
Dickens who, by my calculations was not going to eat his piece of cake,
because he had been dead for 115 years, Professor Schultes told me he
was in need of a student assistant, and asked me if I would like the job.

A few days later, I showed up at the Peabody Museum as he had
directed, wandered past a stuffed display of the last Passenger Pigeon
(which, rumor had it, had been shot by a Harvard expedition), and found
Professor Schultes who immediately put me to work cataloging ethnobotanical specimens, which included among other things a cake of raw
opium which had lain on a shelf unnoticed for some 60 years and a torti-
lla dating from 1897.

Before the day was over, I knew that: 1) Professor Schultes was
world-famous in botanical circles as the "Father of Ethnobotany." 2) Ethnobotany was the scientific study of how people used plants. 3) Professor
Schultes had spent years living in the jungles of Central and South America collecting plant specimens and learning from the people who lived in
the jungle how those plants were used. 4) Professor Schultes' specialty
was hallucinogenic plants and their uses, and he had been the first person
to bring *ayahuasca* to the attention of Europeans. 5) That photo of the
guy on the wall dressed in a loin cloth having hallucinogenic snuff being
blown up his nose by two half-naked men who were only wearing feath-
ers and penis gourds was the same person as the Harvard professor in
the three-piece, tweed suit who had hired me to be his student assistant.

This time there was no sudden revelation. Only gradually, as I worked in the Harvard ethnobotanical collection, did I realize the final things I needed do to become a writer: I needed to live like Professor Schultes in some remote location beyond the comforts of civilization. I needed odd, unpredictable experiences. I needed the ecstasy and terror of nature in its original state. I needed to find a place on this planet where trees outnumbered people. In short, I needed danger, and I needed to survive it.

What I didn't need to do was sample hallucinogens. Professor Schultes had presented me with an entire footlocker of *Banisteriopsis caapi*—the main ingredient in *ayahuasca*—to classify, but I was never seriously tempted to concoct a brew of the famous "black drink." From what I had read, and from what I learned when I listened to him lecture, fever had already given me some of the gifts people seek when they deliberately set out to alter their perceptions of reality, and it had done so without destroying my brain or leaving me addicted to any drug more potent than chocolate.

The summer after I graduated from Harvard, I went to Costa Rica to a place where trees, mosquitoes, and possibly poisonous snakes, outnumbered people. For the next six years I lived off and on at the University of Michigan and at a remote field station in the middle of the jungle. Sometime during those six years, I became a poet. All the pieces were in place: vision, craft, subject, a wider world, time to write, and the means to do so without having to worry about frozen ink (although malaria was always a consideration). Yet until I was well into my fifties, the jungle itself was not the subject of my poetry. It was instead the silent muse behind them, the place where I found the unspoken and non-human; and where, far from civilization, I could contemplate the mysteries of what lies inside human beings both below and above 106°.

Indigo Moor

A Long Overdue Apology

Dear Mrs. Petty,

I am sorry for the frustration I caused you. From this vantage point decades in the future, I see our interactions as cinematic, a horrible retelling of a trite film: science teacher in a white, Southern elementary school discovers gifted black student from a broken home. A rough, but antagonistic, friendship forms, as much armed truce as respect. The ten-year-old child, played on screen by a version of me with better posture and straighter teeth, eventually trusts the teacher and rises to valedictorian of his class. (We didn't have valedictorians back then, but the critics will forgive this license.) Cut to twenty years later. You are retiring. Alone in your classroom. The two decades have not been kind. Budget cuts, crowded classrooms, students more interested in their phones than books. You pack up a crate of all your possessions, surprisingly light considering the weight of the knowledge you have poured into your teachings.

Suddenly, a tall form appears at your open door. It's that one black student everyone told you not to waste time on. You've followed his career through Howard, through MIT, through numerous awards. He's returned at this crucial juncture of your life when you need someone to validate your years of selfless devotion. A tearful reunion as he takes the crate from your trembling hands.

"Let me carry you for a while," he says.

No. Not quite right.

He says, "Let me take that load."

Yes, that sounds like something he would say. As he steps aside to let you pass, a little girl, achingly beautiful, appears, as if by magic, in the door frame. You kneel, one hand on the doorknob to protect knees that have carried the weight of hundreds of children's dreams. You're surprised, but not shocked, to discover she shares your name. When she says, *"I'm not so good at school."* You smile knowingly and say, "let me tell you about your father."

Fade to black.

Unfortunately, the documentary version of my time with you is anything but uplifting. I was aware of how the rest of the class perceived me, perceived all the black students bussed to your neighborhood. I was not broken in the way you think. Are you familiar with the Japanese art form, Kintsugi? Pottery is broken, then reassembled using gold as the binding agent. The idea is not to hide the imperfections but to embrace them. My family was a lot like that. Except we repeated the breaking process every few years, reinventing the vase in ways that helped us cope or, at least, tolerate the pressures of living in the South. I came out of one of those jagged reattachments. No amount of gold could disguise my ill-fit to my religious, working-class upbringing. I read a lot, mostly horror and mystery. Even though my core was R&B, gospel, and funk, I cherished everything from country to jazz. When not engaged in football or basketball, I painted and sketched in secret. I didn't exactly turn my back on God, but I did step around him as if he were a stranger I was forced to pass in a dimly-lit alley. I lived a strangely hermetic life for someone surrounded by family.

You were the first person to recognize that I had more than my share of concrete intelligence. That numbers and postulates, equations and solutions, all obeyed me. Think of it as cilantro. To some, it tastes like soap. To me, math and science were the spice that made the universe palatable. Even then, I could untangle a knot of equations until they were straight as a desert horizon. During our first class, you sparkled when I pronounced *mitochondria* correctly on the first try. If I had known the pain that pronunciation would herald, I would have butchered it, as I eventually did your hopes of mentoring me.

I'm writing to you because I want to discuss the day you broke me. My family lived down Beatties Ford road. In those days, "down Beatties Ford road" carried the same dark inferences as telling someone from California that you are "from the South." Riding the bus to your school every day was like crossing dimensions. Your neighborhood was a forbidden zone for anyone who shared a legacy of racial trauma. The white students and their parents stared at our bus as we passed. We stared back through tightly closed windows, as unsure as they were as to what this crosstown bussing would mean. In my mind, I could see their fists clench and unclench on all they feared but would not say to us. Weeks after the novelty of looking for them wore off, I spent the bus rides with my head against the window, nuzzled against the coolness of Fall. The wind whistling through the cracked rubber of the seals drummed the clamor of the other passengers to silence. Like most mornings, I was half asleep or trying to get there, when I finally relaxed enough for the gate to my fantasy world to open.

And I was gone. As simple as that. Imagination was my private cosmos, and I could disappear, literally, at the speed of thought. Today, I was aboard a sentient spaceship escaping a relentless demolition crew sent to dismantle it. The spaceship was old, a relic from a past age, the last of its design. It plotted long, slow courses through the galaxy, often stopping to reorient itself with nearby planets and stars. It was an all-consuming fantasy, full of twists and turns. I could live all day in this universe, inventing and reinventing adventures for this ship. Unfortunately, that is what I tried to do.

All the kids in your class hated the recorded science lessons you forced upon us. All except me. I loved each one. Primarily because I never listened to any of them. They were my savior from your incessant hovering over me, your hopeful gaze. It was no secret that I was your favorite student. For me, that was a nightmare. Every day, you wandered the aisles in mid-lecture, brushing the tip of your fingers against knees and elbows, prompting us to be mindful of the space we occupied. Each time you paused to ask us questions, you were at my desk, hand on my shoulder, as if I were a lodestone, my magnetic field forcing you out of orbit. Even when I was quiet, when I had no answer to give, I felt pressured to do so. That each hand on my shoulder was my cue to take stage and shine. From that first week as your unwilling protégé, the other students were trying to figure out this strangeness. Like an unsolvable puzzle constantly shoved in their faces, it eventually became easier to despise me. Over the months, I ignored their side glances and condescension, but it still hurt.

I hated your class.

That day's lecture was on the wonderful world of photosynthesis. But I had my own wonderful world. You didn't believe in assigned seating, so I sat down in the back of the class, in the corner, near the extra textbooks gathering dust on a shelf. And I continued my daydream, working through the plight of my spaceship.

I pressed my hands to my ears to block out the monotone dirge from the reel tape. The half-dead voice ran roughshod across my nerves, trying to pull me back to your class. I closed my eyes so tightly solar flares burst behind my eyelids, becoming explosions from the demolition crew attempting to shoot the spaceship down. The fantasy deepened; grew with the attention I gave it. The spaceship's navigation array had been sabotaged, damaging its ability to plot courses. A dying passenger, escaped from a top-secret research facility, had hidden an experimental device aboard that allowed brief jumps through time, up to 30 seconds in the past. But the device was malfunctioning, taking the navigation array with it. The demolition crew chasing the ship was actually a highly specialized retrieval squad from the secret facility, ordered to get the device back. At any cost. Even if it had to dissect the ship to do so. Consumed by my thoughts, I never heard you rise from your chair and come down the aisle to my desk. When you touched my shoulder, the ship exploded.

I don't blame you for what happened. I fully remember what I was like as a student: unfocused, untethered, easily distracted. You must have been horrified that I turned out to be what everyone else in the class expected: a black child from *down Beatties Ford road* who had no business in the same class as them. Again, I apologize for the time you wasted trying to prove them and their parents wrong. I can only guess at the effect of this demonstrative shattering of your faith, only imagine your shame. But I don't have to imagine my own. I didn't look up, so I never saw the look on your face. Your shoes. They were the black ones, the imitation of 1950s wingtips with the grey bobby socks. You kept your hand on my shoulder, speaking not to me, but to the rest of the class.

"I can always tell when a student will be with me next year."

Mrs. Petty, I wasn't a bad kid. I was simply a lost child who invented stories and lived in them. Your threat shamed me and caused me to retreat into a shell. But not for the reason you think. More than failing your class, I feared being shown in a negative spotlight. My terror was of anyone seeing that I also knew I didn't belong. As far as the movie version of this story goes, the rest of the school year was decidedly anticlimactic. I finished all my assignments on time. When you asked questions, I answered as many as I could, eyes glued to you, sitting erect in my chair. I moved to the front of the class where I couldn't see anyone looking at me.

I never found out what happened to that ship.

It took years to regain the confidence to daydream as freely as before I met you. Twenty-six years, to be exact. My fantasies retreated to crevices, coming out only when the light of day waned when no one else could witness me lost in thought and turn on a spotlight. But I wasn't alone. During this great divide between my conscious and subconscious selves, many people whom I now consider inspirations were mentoring me in my growth.

Ed Booker, my history teacher at Coulwood Junior High, who rode a motorcycle, protested Vietnam, gave me my first other-world novel that wasn't Science Fiction. It had a cover with a frenzied barbarian riding the shoulders of an apelike creature that was trying to kill him. Both the artist, Frank Frazetta, and the writer, Robert E, Howard, send tingles through me when I think of them. I secretly wondered if I could put my own worlds on paper, make them as vibrant. An English teacher with green hair—that everyone except me knew was a toupee—introduced me to *Lord of the Flies*. I didn't understand why those children were ridiculed, instead of pitied. *Of Human Bondage, East of Eden*. Both sparked my empathy for suffering, laboring under the subjugation of pain and expectations. I found Langston Hughes in the library, and he mentored my first timid understandings of poetry. "A Dream Deferred" shone through me like the first match that drives away the dark. I had never written a poem in my life, but I thought I could open a journal and pour myself into it.

In high school, my daydreaming reemerged, like an animal buried for days in a collapsed mine: ravenous, hungry. For no reason I can explain, I began writing. My grades plummeted, but my satisfaction with myself rose. Because my intelligence occasionally resurfaced like a seal rising for air, I was relegated to all the Advanced Placement classes. After two years, my English teacher, Jean Avery, presented me as Editor of the Pegasus Literary Magazine. She is still one of my definitions of God. For the first time, I openly dreamed of life as a writer.

But old scars, like old fears, don't fade easily. I told my guidance counselor about my dream of being a writer. Knowing no examples of successful writers, much less black ones, she redirected my river of hope from Liberal Arts colleges to an engineering track at NC State. It wasn't a difficult push. Artistic children with no guidance or direction are targets for those who know better than they do. Besides, the child who abandoned that rocket ship when it needed him most was still in me, always willing to hide from the light.

How do I explain the skipping years? Imagine an immense record album containing all your favorite songs, hundreds of tunes. Now imagine yourself as a stunted needle, worn down by the truncated thing that should be your soul. You stutter and trip across the tracks, skipping at the wrong times, never finding continuity in life. Many of the songs are beautiful: the birth of your children; getting married. Some are tragic: you are a horrible student; you wash out of NC State; join the Navy. Some songs are as eerily serendipitous as a Twilight Zone episode: because of your electronics background in the Navy, Intel hires you, and you spend 20 years as an engineer.

Yes, Mrs. Petty, you were right. I still have a strong affinity for math and science. But my constant struggle to define myself in ways that ignored my creativity stunted me. I love my children, loved my marriage, tolerated my job. But I was hollow. An outsider in my own actions, robbed of being a full participant in my life. I was no longer able to see that the vase was broken, had lost the knack for repair. One day, I woke up in Cambridge, MA, on my way to divorce, with knowledge of being a father, a husband, an engineer, and little else. I had skipped through thousands of songs, never having a chance to sing any of them with my voice.

As I conclude this apology, typing slowly with, at most, three fingers since typing was yet another class that didn't hold my attention, I want to describe my surroundings. It's 2019. I'm renting a very large mid-century home in Sacramento, CA. I have lived in this house through eight Halloweens, my favorite holiday. I'm 54 years old, lying on my side in bed, typing, listening to the rain, typing some more. It's early spring, but still a little cold for my taste. When I finally get up to make some tea, I will slip on Bunny Slippers, ones with big teeth like the vicious rabbit in The Search for the Holy Grail. Later today, I will drive down to San Jose to continue a lucrative engineering consulting job. Yes, I am *still* an engineer. But even though I am very good at it, that profession means little to me. It represents a small niche in my life, a crevice much like the one that I used to force my imagination to crawl into and hide. Allow me to introduce myself.

My name is Indigo Moor. I am the Poet Laureate of Sacramento. I am also a scriptwriter and author. I have written three books of poetry, including *Through the Stonecutter's Window* (2010), which won Northwestern University Press's *Cave Canem* prize. As with my first book, *Tap-Root* (2008), my 2017 release, *In the Room of Thirsts & Hungers*, is an Editor's Select choice from Main Street Rag. Last year, I collaborated with visual artist Barry Ebner to produce the poetry / abstract art book, *Fragments.*

I teach creative writing at the Stonecoast MFA Program, where I graduated in 2012 with an MFA in poetry, fiction, and scriptwriting. I am on the advisory boards for the Sacramento Poetry Center and Modesto Stanislaus Poetry Center, a *Cave Canem* fellow, the resident artist at *916 ink,* and a graduate member of the Artist's Residency Institute for Teaching Artists. Three of my short plays, *Harvest, Shuffling,* and *The Red and Yellow Quartet* debuted at the *60 Million Plus Theatre*'s Spring Playwright's festival. My full-length stage play, *Live! at the Excelsior,* was a finalist for the *Images Theatre Playwright Award* and was optioned for a full-length film.

I could go on, but you get my point. My engineering work is only important in one respect: it allows me to be my own private patron. I am a man who lives by writing down what is in his head. Engineering only pays the bills. I am focused on the arts beyond most imaginings. I am driven and extremely ambitious. You would not recognize me.

In Cambridge, MA briefly separated from my children and all I had been, I was forced to rediscover myself. In a catharsis that spanned two years, I gave myself over to writing. From a Bible Belt perspective, you could say I was baptized in the Komunyakaa river. swam with Dove, scratched myself running through the briar patches of Dawes, Finney, and Toomer. I rode the Shore to Cassells and many, many more. I literally wrote myself into being. I broke myself and reassembled the pieces over and over, until I understood every inch of my being in painful brightness, in exquisite gold. Yes, this process is never-ending. But, each year, I find the breaking process less traumatic, the cracks a little less noticeable. The pieces fit together so tightly even I can't find the seams. Mrs. Petty. I am sorry to say you really were wasting your time. I was never going to be a scientist, or biologist, or a mathematician for a very simple reason.

I'm a writer. And anything that makes it difficult for me to write, makes it difficult for me to breathe. I have spent the last 19 years learning to incorporate all I love into my writing world, letting all the songs work with each other. For this, I don't owe an apology to you or anyone else.

Understand, this letter is not a rebuke. I'm not upset with you. I'm writing because I left something in your class, and I need it back. My bedroom is next to my office. A large room with wall-to-wall bookcases, where most of my work, if not begun, is completed. I must be quick now. I can already feel the walls shaking, books jostling, toppling off the shelves. As I said, there is always another vase to break. And, as the rumbling in my office rises to a dull roar, I know I've found what I left behind in your class.

Goodbye, Mrs. Petty. I've got a spaceship to catch.

Signed,

Me

Kim Shuck

Maybe the Pepperwood Tree Taught Me to Write

IN MANY WAYS ASKING ME HOW I BECAME a poet is like asking a caterpillar how it walks, suddenly I can't write about it. I tried to remember when I first called myself a poet. I mean, I know that I am one. It says so on my business card. It says so in my CV. You can't ask for better verification than being the 7th Poet Laureate of San Francisco. At the same time, I've never needed that kind of affirmation for anything else, it makes me a bit uncomfortable if I'm honest. Do I pretend that it was all ordained? Shall I tell my story with a cheeky wink of self-satisfaction because we now know how it worked out? Should I admit that I think it's all a big misunderstanding?

Trying to make sense:

Baby hands on the sink in grandma's house, having a bath. Pretending I was driving an old-fashioned roadster made of bubbles. Mistaking the word 'spoon' for the word 'school'. There were Grandpa's fancy European handwriting and the stories about the ghost in the upstairs room. Not knowing which words were in what language.

In nursery school I stood at the top of the outside stairs in a Victorian broad brimmed hat, a string of pearls and a lace mini dress, and black leather button up shoes. Watching the boys play, naked in a mud puddle. No girls. I strip to the pearls and wade in.

I call mom, ask her when I started writing:

"Wow!" But she gives it a try. "You loved books and most children's books are poems, or at least they rhyme. I don't know. I imagine you started in first grade." She reminds me of a poem I wrote about a woman dying in her herb garden. I find out that she (read this for everyone in the family) thought that this poem was about grandma. It was actually about an Edwardian woman we'd now call a botanist, but I leave it. "You used to make tiny books all of the time."

Remembering a great hippy toy store from the late 60s. It sold tiny books in sets and I wanted them so I made little books. Now I make books. Maybe this is the balloon string I was looking for.

> Crawling all over the playground in Golden Gate Park
> The two person swings
> The carousel
> Crawling all over the trains at the SF Zoo
> Were they at the zoo or the playground?
> Maybe zoo
> The little child sized houses
> I'm sure that those were in the zoo
> I still have my blue zoo key
> Cotton candy in my hair
> It was the 60s

Dad had a drawing and what he thought was my first poem pinned up next to his tool bench in the basement. I don't know that I wrote that piece. I may have copied it, some school thing.

> Under the table with crayons listening to poets with Carol Lee
> Blue poem / crayon
> Poem at the Mission Cultural Center
> Poem somewhere in North Beach
> Poem at the smaller version of Modern Times Bookstore
> Poem at City Lights Bookstore
> I knew poets early

All of that is real. There were obviously other things going on. I have no idea how often we went to the park or the zoo. My grandma taught me to crochet. Ok, let's be clearer about that: my grandmother was a "no idle hands" kind of woman. She crocheted, knitted to a lesser degree, made handmade lace, went through a quilting phase, made jam, planted things like carrots. She and grandpa were seriously frugal and therefore creative. I have a memory of cookies flavored with old Halloween candy. Creativity also has a fail rate. I had homemade toys because she preferred not to throw anything away. I learned those things because they were happening near me and I wanted to know how everything worked.

Mom says, "You were always very verbal."

Dad took me to see a piece of jade that was much larger than me. It was at a gem and mineral show in Golden Gate Park and he also gave me thirty cents to buy something. I got three things: a section of crinoid, a tiny tri-lobite and a piece of rose quartz. That last was because every woman in my mom's family is somehow named rose or a variation of rose.

How is everyone not just curious about everything? Is that the part in me that's broken in a way that makes me poet?

Should I talk about the math? The physics? I don't remember when I started thinking about the nature of things.

One night it sounded as if the back yard was on fire, there was this crackling and popping. Dad went outside to see, then called us all out. The tree in our neighbor's yard was making the noise, all of its seedpods cracking open and throwing tiny black seeds everywhere. For the next few weeks, I collected seeds and kept them in a walnut shell. Was that collecting the same as making a poem?

There was a war on. I think I should mention that. My dad had been on the Ticonderoga, an aircraft carrier, during the Gulf of Tonkin incident. I was aware of the war but not as aware of it as I was of the mica in the soil on our hill, the giant blackberry bramble in the corner of the yard and watching the blackberries get ripe. There was also a toad I remember as gigantic. He wasn't a pet, just lived in the yard.

I used to think that it should be possible to read a book by the energy of all of the little cloud formations of atoms. I think someone explained matter to me as a bunch of tiny clocks packed very close together. Maybe they said that things went round and round like clocks, or clocks that went around in all directions at once. I don't remember when I realized that color and matter were mostly imagination. Now all of this makes me seem like a fairly joyful child or maybe a wise child, at the time I think I was just understood as strange. You try telling other first graders, or worse yet the adults, that since there was less stuff in matter than we thought, we should be able to move through it somehow. Yep, I was strange. Not in an ultimately useful way either, I was just endlessly and obsessively curious about most things.

Books
Libraries

There was a time when I'd read everything in the children's sections of three local libraries. Then I started on the books for grown ups.

The Noe Valley Library had a display of a grouping of Ruth Asawa's knotless netted structures. Ruth was someone we knew, working in a technique my little handwork capable self-understood, the work displayed in a place I loved. That bit is probably important. Art is a possibility.

Let's get real it was San Francisco.

I haven't yet mentioned that my father is Indigenous. At the time he was an Indian (sorry, that's a joke with a very small hit zone but I'm leaving it there). Dad is Cherokee. In the 60s and 70s my father was one of the most beautiful men you'd ever see. I am very light skinned so the vibe of the time was less striking for me. For my father it must have been like attending your own funeral day after day. Rumor was that we were all dead. Then MIA. Dad, as I mentioned, was in the Navy. He's a genius in a world where that word is overused.

> He's a genius in a world where that word is overused. No college,
> electronics, engineer, retired as a scientist for IBM, brown . . . .

I could not be prouder of my dad. He's got flaws but I'm going to leave them out. Does watching family members suffer being misunderstood help one to find a poetic voice? I'm sure that there's a school of thought where that is a big yes. It does normalize being incomprehensible. Anyway, most women I met for at least two decades had a crush on my dad, it was, at one point, a recognized lifestyle.

Among all of those books I was reading there were Berlitz language courses. I have not mastered all of the languages I studied, but I was interested in the links and disconnects between the puzzle of words. My grandparents spoke an archaic form of Polish. My great gran on the other side spoke Cherokee. The dominant form of Chinese in San Francisco was Cantonese. Many of our friends spoke Spanish, including our friend Betty (in another world my godmother) who was from San Salvador and therefore spoke a very particular kind of Spanish. One of grandma's friends was Swiss. I was surrounded by a maze of words and wordlings. People forget that San Francisco was like that. People ignore that San Francisco is like that now.

Struck by a memory of a High School teacher newly arrived from Boston who assured me that there was no evidence of Spanish colonialism in San Francisco.

> San Pancho
> Shaking my head
> People see what they want to

This table I'm sitting at is made up of clouds of particles and the supposed surface is an agreement we make with reality.

What is the effect of being required to memorize nonsense about your own home cultures for the purpose of passing grades in school? It was the cold war and the Polish had mostly vanished from schoolbooks. Indigenous people were, reportedly, all gone. Then I'd go home and eat Polish food and talk to my Cherokee dad. I suppose you either learn that you don't exist, or that you are an exception and take a step sideways.

Pow Wow friendship dances are all sidesteps. This is my agreement with reality.

> Buying one piece of very fancy chocolate in Carmel
> Playing at being roadie for a friend's mom
> Pulling off of the freeway to swim in the American River
> Fantasy role-playing games: dice, paper, pencils, charts, cookies
> School jerks, many of them the teachers
> Heart friend who has fallen away, that still hurts too much, moving on

High school poetry teacher told me my writing was too self-referential to ever really work

My dad's mom didn't like that my poems don't rhyme

Then Carol Lee Sanchez, the famous Laguna poet, my heroine, said, "Kim has a poem. Read your poem, Kim." Is that when I became a poet?

Having children gave me permission to make furniture forts and tea parties and the four of us reading to one another every night. If I'm a poet, I was already a poet by then.

This may not be true of everyone but I think that I become a poet every day. The thing that makes me curious, the thing that snags my attention, the meditation the idée fixe, the tool that will pull words out of ideas. Maybe I just write myself every day, make myself real. It is an act of audacity, writing a poem, standing to read the poem, being filmed reading the poem. It doesn't always work. I aim for about a 25% success rate, which is probably an indication of arrogance. The way that I write, I couldn't have learned it in school. I'm not even sure that I could teach it. I have sat for hours reading books in trees. One of my favorite trees is a bay laurel that lives in my parents' yard. Out here they call them pepperwood trees, maybe she taught me to be a poet.

Philip F. Clark

Sustain Wonder

In the deepest hour of the night, confess to yourself that you would die
if you were forbidden to write. And look deep into your heart where it
spreads its roots, the answer, and ask yourself, must I write?

—Rainer Maria Rilke, *Letters to a Young Poet*

ALL WRITERS, WHETHER THEY COME to their work young, or after many
years, at some point ask the inevitable question that Rilke speaks of,
'Must I write?' And note that Rilke does not say, 'should,' or 'can'; he
admits that the need to write is already there. The journey for the writer
is to get to 'I must.' It is a long travel for most. As a poet and teacher who
came to writing and teaching later in life, my perspective is always two-
fold: that of what I was given to get me where I am, but also what I can
give back, now that I have attained them.

In my life, I can directly attest that I came to writing by reading. I can
remember distinctly, watching, and listening to my father read—constantly; every morning, often before dawn, I would wake early, hear him
turning pages of whatever book he had a small number of hours to read
before work. This image inspired one of my first poems, many years
later. But that first experience of my father's deep commitment to books
was an impetus to do the same. And I did; as I grew, I would have conversations with him about what he read, why he read. What authors he
enjoyed most (as a Merchant Marine during the war, he loved naval, military history, and travel, novels, biographies: Herman Wouk, Shelby Foote,
James Clavell, James Michener). These books deeply engaged him. And
it was that engagement that so compelled me—even when I knew my
reading tastes would not be his. Yet, I also had an older sister, who also
read deeply and more widely. It was she who brought me to the plays and
sonnets of Shakespeare, the Classics, the novels of Henry James, James

Baldwin, Faulkner, the plays of Tennessee Williams, Jean Rhys, Edith Wharton, the poetry of Emily Dickinson, Robert Frost, William Carlos Williams, W. H. Auden, Philip Larkin, Sylvia Plath. She opened up reading as a vast possibility for me that was more than just the art of it, but the goal to think about developing writing as well. Those possibilities, that over many years, would find a place in my life, as a writer and teacher.

Those two early mentors—cicerones in the best sense—gave me a foundation that I have built upon since. The only other singular time in my life of such mentorship was during my study at Fordham University, where I found another mentor, Dr. Eva Stadler, while studying a class called 'The Novel.' It was she, who deepened even more my love of reading and spurred my interest in teaching, in a way that to this day, I call upon as a teacher, poet, and editor myself. To this day, I can feel the chill up my spine at the last paragraphs of *Middlemarch* and *The Dead*. I still have Welleck and Warren's *Theory of Literature*, the first critical study she introduced me to. Suddenly, reading became three-dimensional, and not just a mirror—a new door. And as Emily Dickinson said, "The Soul should always stand ajar, ready to welcome the ecstatic experience . . . ".

And I think of these things—mentorship, attention, acknowledgment—I know how important they were to me as I was starting seriously to write poetry. Before my first collection was published, I was already teaching at City College, pursuing an MFA in Creative Writing. And so, I was both student and instructor, needing to learn, as well as needing to give back what I learned. In the confluence of both I have come to learn that a young writer, an emerging poet, needs, above all, attention. The attention that is specific to that writer alone, unlike any other. Someone who will say, "I understand what you see," as well as "I will help you become who you want to be. I see you and will give you the tools to become that poet." I am reminded of the student in one of my technical writing classes who 'secretly' wrote poems in the back of the room. When I asked him to show me some of his work, I was astounded at his talent. Being a biology major, he had never pursued this 'play,' seriously, in his word for it.

More than at any other time, writing of every genre, but especially poetry, has expanded—young writers have vast opportunities to submit work, develop their art, and network among colleagues, if they take the chance to do so. Encouragement is needed, but finding a community is integral. The problem is how to separate the many choices people now have to find the few most relevant voices. Young writers must be truants at some point: to wend away from the crowd and begin listening to themselves. It is the crux of Rilke's words of how solitude engenders a consciousness to oneself, and therefore an honesty of truth in their work. They need to find the tools of context, deep reading, and the understanding of elemental skills that must develop their writing: Form, structure, imagery, idea. But above all, they must have someone who believes in their work and is constant in encouragement—of sustaining wonder.

Without question, with the ease and access to opportunity that young writers now have, all the communities that can instill inspiration and compel first chances, this is a time that can seem limitless. Yet, it is a time when we cannot forget the 'secret' writers in the back of rooms, simply looking for someone to notice their singularity. The journey of writers, especially young writers, is to grow toward that ecstatic experience, but also toward trust—that singular trust in themselves that will enable them to create with a freedom that comes only after acknowledging and accepting who they are as individuals with unique voices. Using the tools they've learned, they're able to let their voices be not only heard but recognized. It is a metamorphosis, a final becoming. Then they see—or, thankfully, have been shown—that they have gotten to those very words 'I must write.'

"The main thing is this," Grace Paley wrote in 1989, "when you get up in the morning you must take your heart in your two hands. You must do this every morning."

Gail Newman

Alphabets of a Lost Tongue

MY PARENTS AND MOST OF THEIR FRIENDS were immigrants, Polish Holocaust survivors who spoke a mingling of languages—Yiddish, Polish, German, Hebrew. Sometimes their sentences would begin in one language and end in another, the conversation sprinkled with mysterious words that I couldn't understand, sounds that scratched my throat when I tried to imitate, syllables that danced away from me. Polish, my mother said, was a language that could break your tongue.

> I mumble random words, alphabets of a lost
> tongue, alert for the perfect lexicon that will tell me
> who I am, the language that will free me from longing
> and loneliness: *Zaide,* grandfather, *l'chaim,* faith.

Before I was a writer, I was a reader. My mother's father was a journalist who treated her, she said, like a son, taking her with him to political meetings and encouraging her intellectual development. She had the advantage of attending a Jewish school for girls, where she was sheltered from prejudice and encouraged to be smart and accomplished. She loved books and took me frequently to the local library. My ambition was to go through the shelves alphabetically reading every book. Maybe that was the seed of my writing life.

Or maybe the seed resided with my father, a tailor by profession, who could fashion a suit of clothes from start to finish, sew a dress from collar to hem. He would enter a conversation first with a touch of one's sleeve, a comment on the quality of the material. My father was a storyteller who paid attention to detail. When he spoke, he would spin the past into a movie I could see behind my eyes. He talked about his life in Poland before the war, his large family of six siblings, the lakes, and cherry trees of his youth. He spoke of the war in a glazed way, at a distance, the way victims of trauma do when they remember.

He is inside the telling of his story,
his body far away, hidden under a mattress,
jumping off a train into snow,
hiding potatoes in his pockets.
We dug a trench. Then we filled it up.
Every day. Marching there and back
until it was dark. We ate cold soup,
not soup, water. Nothing.

How do we become who we are? I think, surely, my immigrant background was an influence in becoming a writer. Until I started kindergarten, I spoke no English. The demographics of my neighborhood and school were primarily Chicano with a Spanish speaking population, so I was twice removed from a language I could understand. I was isolated and quiet. I remember an incident in second grade when I gave an oral report about my pet and said *kenery* instead of canary, and everyone laughed. My mother cooked an artichoke and declared it inedible because it was too tough. She didn't know to only eat the tender part. Now, as I write, I notice the previous sentence is in my immigrant vernacular, not quite grammatical, not quite *correct*. Perhaps this affords me some freedom as a poet, the ability to experiment with language, to write outside the box. Dialogue, conversation, has always been part of my poetry. I am attracted to speech, to the music of dialects.

Gai platz, the uncles would shout in unison, no one
listening. *Gai mit dein kop in drerd,*
Summer nights or in the kitchen when the *kinder* were pretending
sleep, they'd murmur *Gedenkst?* Remember?
and their voices would take on a tone
. . . . the English would fade away like smoke
until only the Yiddish remained, and we were foreigners
in our own houses, with strangers for parents.

I always felt my family had a story and that perhaps it was my obligation, my destiny and desire to tell it. But I wasn't at first drawn to poetry. I thought I might write a novel or a memoir. Although poetry, I felt, had an emotional depth, a precision I couldn't find elsewhere. I didn't know I could write poetry. I thought it was for academics, that I wasn't educated or smart enough to be a poet.

Los Angeles was a sprawling desert where I felt lost. I moved to San Francisco to find a community of writers, just in time for the arrival of the Women's Movement that was barreling around the corner, and it hit me head on. Women began to publish poets who had been excluded from recognition. I was an English Lit major, and we were required to read the Norton Anthology of English Literature, the academic bible, which consisted of primarily white male writers. Women began to protest by publishing their own small presses and magazines—Kelsey Street Press in Berkeley, *Lilith*, *Calyx*. Anthologies, including *No More Masks* edited by Ellen Bass, introduced me to Anne Sexton, Gwendolyn Brooks, Adrienne Rich, Nikki Giovanni, and so many others. These poets spoke to me in an intimate, visceral way that I hadn't experienced before.

I took a class at Intersection for the Arts in North Beach with Diane di Prima. I began to write poetry secretly in my journal. I must have slipped the secret to my roommate because she told her friend, Stephanie Mines, a local poet who ran a women's workshop and salon in her storefront apartment in Noe Valley. Stephanie asked me to join and when I did, I suddenly had a community, a poetry family who would listen, comment, and encourage. We read at bookstores, contributed to Stephanie's Noe Valley Anthology and began to stretch in confidence and craft. I joined a women's poetry workshop with Diane di Prima at Intersection for the Arts in North Beach. With a friend, I launched a magazine, *Room, A Women's Literary Journal*. To get started, we produced a benefit reading with Stephanie Mines, Kathleen Fraser, Susan Griffin, and Judy Grahn. The cost of admission was about $3.00, and the room was packed! We went on to publish the early work of Sharon Olds and Kay Ryan. We published older poets who had been overlooked and interviews, including one with Mary Mackey. I enrolled in a Feminist Poetics course with Kathleen Fraser, who subsequently wrote a curriculum book that included poetry and essays by the women in our class. I had found my people and my place.

The next big event in my writing life was the discovery of California Poets in the Schools. I had gone on in college to get a teaching credential, because what else, I thought, could a woman do for a living? I loved working with children, but I felt uncomfortable and unsatisfied. Through news from the grapevine, I found myself at meeting with Carol Lee Sanchez. Poet-teachers sat on the floor and leaned against the walls drinking coffee and smoking cigarettes. I was welcomed and encouraged to become a poet-teacher—which I did. My teaching life has been parallel to my writing life, and one has informed the other.

My new book, *Blood Memory*, tells my parent's story. Why did it take so long to write the story that was inside me? I became a poet, a teacher, a wife. I learned to cook and make a garden. I made a child. I went to school meetings, wrote grants, bought a dining table, a set of wine glasses, a house. And still, I did not write my family's story. Why? I tried when I was young and could not do it. I was discouraged by others, who said, *So much had been written about the Holocaust already.* As if it was irrelevant, old news. I did not know how to write about the unspeakable. I had to learn to step back and let the story unfold without interference, to keep my emotions leashed, so the reader could respond-feel, see, be moved or horrified or hopeful.

When my father died, I began to write about him. The flood gates were open. I went to Poland with my husband and The March of the Living to find the past. I found my father's house and his work papers from the Lodz Ghetto. I went inside the run-down building in Lodz that was once the ghetto where my mother lived in one room with her brother and my grandmother. I went to the graveyard in Auschwitz where my grandmother was buried. I saw the forest where the ashes of the dead fell. I thought about my childhood.

> they'd murmur *Gedenkst* . . .
> and the English would fade away like smoke
> until only the Yiddish remained, and we were foreigners
> in our own houses, with strangers for parents.

Some days, now, I can't believe the state of the world. It seems we haven't come as far as we thought. Through this time of Pandemic, bigotry, global warming, I keep my parent's stories close to my heart. I think of them every day—what they went through, how they survived.

I think about poetry, kindness, the earth. Resilience. How much we have of beauty. Why we need to remember the past. Elie Wiesel said—

> *Whoever listens to a witness, becomes a witness.*

Basil King

The Past is as Present as I Want the Future to Be

IF AS A YOUNG MAN a gallery or galleries had been interested in showing my paintings, I would have had no time to think about writing. I would have painted and been involved with maintaining my reputation. Alas, there were many promises to show my paintings, but they all came to naught. I was fifty years old when in desperation I began to write. I had been painting since I was fourteen. At Black Mountain College I took classes with Olson, Duncan and Creeley. But if I hadn't been painting all these years, I would never have known that I put disparate things together.

[Pause]

I was in a carpenter's shop and the floor was strewn with shavings. The shavings were the remains of paintings and drawings from the past. In the dream I picked up handfuls of shavings with works from the cave to the present. They were unfinished. I held them in my hands and slowly while working I began to know what to do to put disparate things together.

[Pause]

Dreams channel history and history has the power to turn things upside down. I have been haunted by two experiences one I had at the age of six and one at seven that to this day inform how I feel I am supposed to be in the world.

[Pause]

Memory recalls the traumas. Memory recalls and I pause and digest. Memory says there is no great distance between right and wrong, good or bad, only a thin line separates the two. I am obliged to repeat I love to paint, and I love to write poetry.

[Pause]

We live in a house on 4th Street in Brooklyn. I have been working on a new series of drawing and painting I call 4th Street. I painted a large portrait of "A Snow Man on 4th Street." It has a very disturbing presence. I wasn't sure of where it came from. What was it telling me? I wasn't able to paint for weeks. A few days ago, I was scribbling in my sketchpad and a drawing told me.

[Pause]

The Green Man Comes to 4th Street.
Emily's sidewalk
Danny's garden
My forte
My steps
My ladder
Leads to
A description of Green
Paled by Yellow
Eyes
Housed
In a cavity
I am an oar
To Emily's sidewalk
To Danny's garden
My forte
My steps
My ladder
Leads to
A house
Runs
Like water
Runs
One floor
At a time
To Emily's sidewalk
To Danny's garden
My forte

My steps
My ladder
Leads to

[Pause]

Why learn to cross the street? Why remember the first tree I climbed? Why remember my mother and father's faces, the first girl I had a crush on, the Second World War, school. What marks the self from being selfless? Ego, erudition, something you must have, a cup, a knife and fork, knowledge, status. There are days when the sun appears and on other days the clouds bring rain a wet reminder that memory stays and accumulates. What is history?

[Pause]

My MRI tells me that I might have had a stroke when I was still in the womb. I was a Caesarian birth and I was pulled out incorrectly. The loss of oxygen caused damage to the nerves on the right side of my body. It is a mild case of cerebral palsy. To this day blood goes too slowly to my brain.

[Pause]

A very learned lady once told me. "If I wanted to I could learn to play the violin by turning the violin around and using my damaged right hand to bow." It's a wonderful compliment.

[Pause]

I am not a selfie who takes refuge in behavior that contradicts humility. What is the norm? I question the legitimacy of the norm. It is a behavior that questions nothing and is the enemy of poetry. Hear the undertow: brevity takes its toll.

[Pause]

The past is as present as I want the future to be. It is on behalf of this that I contribute my painting and my poetry.

Sandy
McIntosh

David
Lehman

Jason
McCall

Denise
Low

Jane
Hirshfield

Denise
Duhamel

Phillip
Lopate

David Lehman

Opening Shot

I. WHITMAN IN THE ELEVENTH GRADE

In high school I read "Song of Myself" in a course in American literature that began with the poets who had three names (William Cullen Bryant, Oliver Wendell Holmes, Julia Ward Howe, John Greenleaf Whittier,
James Russell Lowell, Henry Wadsworth Longfellow) and never reached
the moderns who went by their initials (T. S. Eliot, W. H. Auden). In that
context it meant something that Whitman used no middle name and only
a shortened version of his forename. I liked this fellow who was "mad
for it to be in contact with me," whether "it" stood for nature, the grass,
a particular person, a brook—that was how I felt, too, in my more unin-
hibited moments. I liked the anthology excerpts so much I bought, with
fool's luck, a thin paperback of *Leaves of Grass* that called itself the "original edition," edited by Malcolm Cowley. To this day I maintain that the
1855 edition is the greatest version of this great American poem, which
Whitman revised often and not always for the better.

Back in the eleventh grade, I didn't dislike Bryant's "Thanatopsis."
That poem gave me something to brood on. It appealed to me as a reader.
Whitman, however, appealed to the poet in me, the part of me that I
wasn't aware of until then. Whitman's language was the first thing that
drew me to him, his diction, and then his caution-to-the-winds indiffer-
ence to metrical models. The language of "Thanatopsis" was not the language I spoke, whereas every leaf of "Song of Myself" announced the
birth of a new language, the American language, mine.

I loved Whitman's extravagance. Everything about "Song of Myself"
was extravagant, but perhaps most especially the self-celebrating "I" of
the poem, "Walt Whitman, an American, one of the roughs, a kosmos."

This character, "Walt Whitman," could fancy himself the poet of the
body and the poet of the soul, the poet of the woman the same as the man.

He was magnificent, magnifying, and magnanimous. He refashioned the American religion in the image of one who preferred the smell of his armpits to prayer, who beheld God everywhere yet could not understand who there could be more wonderful than himself. He was the poet of common sense and the poet of immortality. He was my grandfather, and he assured me there was nothing rank in copulation. Did he contradict himself? Yes, he admitted it freely. Why not? He was large enough to contain the crowd.

Most of all I loved the end of the poem. A summing up takes place here, a reassertion of the metaphoric element that ties everything together. "I bequeath myself to the dirt to grow from the grass I love," he says. "If you want me again look for me under your bootsoles." The visionary Whitman has moments of ecstatic puzzlement when any language fails him: "There is that in me. . . I do not know what it is . . . but I know it is in me." In this mood he names happiness as a noble theme. I loved him as much for that as for his defense of the "barbaric yawp," the untamed dialect of the tribe. And the freedom to contradict himself.

But what chilled me about the end of the poem, what chills me to this day, is its valediction—as if indeed a friend and not a book were departing, or as if that book had a voice and all the attributes of a man, and he was saying goodbye and godspeed because he was about to die and he knew it and was not afraid. At the end of "Ode to a Nightingale" (which I had not read in high school) Keats pauses and salutes the departure of his vision. At the end of "Song of Myself," Whitman says goodbye not to the vision but to the reader. Unlike Keats, he is not plaintive or forlorn. The poem and its author have merged entirely, and the reader has emerged as a new character, "you," who exist as if in fulfillment of a prophecy. "You" witness the withdrawal of the vision but extend it at the same time, for "you" and "I" are one ("every atom belonging to me as good belongs to you"). No period is needed at the end, because all ends are temporary, as death is a temporary condition for the poet who understands it is "lucky" to die and be reborn constantly in the form of a new reader. I was that reader, the "you" to whom he spoke when he stopped "somewhere waiting for you." The knowledge that many others must feel similarly singled-out did nothing to diminish the glory.

II. A PAIR OF ODES

When I was seventeen, I wrote two poems that eventually were published. Both consisted of four lines. To both I gave the title "Ode." I had never heard of Horace or Pindar and didn't know what went into the making of an ode as composed by Jonson, Marvell, Shelley, or Keats. But the word was lovely and in the atmosphere of the 1960s it was okay to break rules, even to be ignorant of what they were.

The first of the odes to be written appeared in a broadsheet published by the poet John Fuller in Oxford, England, summer 1968:

> I asked a fat man,
> Do you enjoy being fat?
> "Yes," he answered,
> that is the only thing that I enjoy.

It pleased me that the last line of this simple poem scanned perfectly as iambic pentameter, as if to demonstrate that it is the natural flow of the English language—what we today might call the default meter.

The second ode made a hit with Columbia University radicals during the campus strike of spring 1968, perhaps because it made people laugh when I read it aloud:

> As long as I live,
> there shall never be
> another Harry
> Truman.

What made me break up the lines as I did? What made me think that these were poems? I don't know the answer to these and other legitimate questions except to say that I let instinct guide me where it will, and in the end, instinct is what we have to fall back on.

III. FRANKLY . . . YOU'RE OKAY

In the first month of my freshman year at Columbia, I wrote a poem nearly every day, often after taking a walk in Fort Tryon Park. What possessed me? Nervous excitement: the excitement of being fully alive, grown to my full height, challenged and stimulated intellectually as never before. In the morning I had classes on Homer, the French resistance in World War II, and the ontological proof of God's existence as set forth by Saint Anselm, refuted by Aquinas, and demolished by Kant. In the afternoon I walked up Sherman Avenue, turned left on Dyckman Street, right on Broadway, and discovered *The New American Poetry*, Donald M. Allen's landmark anthology (1960), at the Inwood branch of the New York Public Library. There was much in that book that spoke to me. The poet who caught my attention and held it the longest was Frank O'Hara, who had, I was soon to learn, died a few months before I read such poems as "Why I Am Not a Painter," "The Day Lady Died," "In Memory of My Feelings," "Ode to Michael Goldberg's "Birth and Other Births," and the poem dated 9 / 17 / 59, which begins *"Khrushchev is coming on the right day!"* The anthology's five other O'Hara poems from 1959 were also given dates as if to say or imply that the writing of poetry was a daily occurrence and that an accumulation of the poems would therefore constitute a chronicle of the poet's many selves. Not until many years later did I adopt my own practice of writing a poem a day and collecting the results in two "journals in poetry," *The Daily Mirror* (2000) and *The Evening Sun* (2002). I was aware of other exemplars of the daily poem: Emily Dickinson, A. R. Ammons, James Schuyler, William Stafford, Robert Bly. But my first inspiration came from Frank O'Hara, O'Hara when he was still a secret, before the academics discovered him.

I bought *Meditations in an Emergency* and *Lunch Poems*, the two O'Hara collections, and read them on the subway. He would have approved. O'Hara was witty, brilliant, erudite, but also down to earth. He was colloquial, he made the life of New York painters and poets seem glamorous. His meditations were as quick and urgent as the time required. Poetry was continuous with his life.

O'Hara dashed off poems on his lunch break. A tabloid headline might trigger the process, or a chance encounter with a friend, a party, a classical symphony on the radio. Nor did you have to wait until you were alone at your desk. The stimulus for a poem could occur in a bar as easily as in a concert hall or museum. Riding the Staten Island Ferry, he jotted down one of his "I do this I do that" poems. Before reading O'Hara's *Lunch Poems* I didn't know it was okay to start a poem with "Lana Turner has collapsed." It was also okay to depart from your daily routine and imagine a conversation with the sun or make sound translations (or pseudo-translations) from the German. O'Hara exemplified a style of freedom; he participated in what came to be called the "tradition of the new" but was also firmly grounded in the traditional sense of tradition.

He knew art, music, French poetry, Russian poetry; incorporated these influences in his poems; and never made you feel stupid if you hadn't before encountered the names that appear in his poems. Verlaine, Bonnard, Hesiod, Brendan Behan, Strega the liqueur, Gauloises and Picayunes the cigarettes, the Five Spot bar, and the pianist Mal Waldron, all show up in "The Day Lady Died." I would wager that more than a few poets sipped Strega after a meal or bought a pack of Gauloises just because of that poem.

O'Hara demonstrated that writing poetry could be as natural an act as talking on the telephone or walking in the street with a friend. Imitating Mayakovsky, he happily puns on his name when he mouths the words of the sun:

> Frankly I wanted to tell you
> I like your poetry. I see a lot
> on my rounds and you're okay. You may
> not be the greatest thing on earth, but
> you're different.

It seems a modest claim to make for oneself, but remember, it is not everyone who gets to be on speaking terms with the sun.

IV. THE SUN AT FIVE O'CLOCK

At Columbia, poetry was my reality. The sun at five o'clock was a poem. I fell in love and it was a poem. I looked straight, hair neatly combed, no beard, and yet I was a poet. I held hands with a girl and lived in a bildungsroman. I read James Joyce and was a poet.

Walking up a steep hill to get to George Washington High School, where I took an evening class in touch typing, I rewrote a poem. As it snowed and the snow fell diagonally across the trees of Fort Tryon Park, I wore a black topcoat, looked in the darkened mirror-like shop windows, and saw Scott Fitzgerald's profile. One Sunday I accompanied David Shapiro to NYU's Loeb Student Center, where Kenneth Koch and John Ashbery read newly discovered poems by their late friend Frank O'Hara, and the subway tokens in my pocket were poems. The forest green V-neck sweater on the couch became a meadow and I had a new poem. By the end of my first year at Columbia, four poems of mine (two in verse, two in prose) had appeared in *Columbia Review*. In June I learned that "The Presidential Years" won the university's Van Rensselaer Prize, and in the fall, it and a second poem ("Traces") were accepted by Tom Clark for *The Paris Review*. That was all I needed. I was a poet and a passenger on a drunken boat. Everything around me, everyone I met, spoke poetry.

V. LESSONS LEARNED

Write any time, any place. Take a little notebook with you. Jot down possible titles, overheard phrases, unexpected similes.

Write prose. All the writing you do helps all the other writing you do. Learn the prose virtues of economy, directness, and clarity. Good journalism or nonfiction writing or speech writing or technical writing can help your poetry. Writing to an editor's specifications, on deadline, with a tight word-count, is a sort of discipline not unlike writing poems in rigorous forms. It teaches you brevity.

I always liked writing captions and headlines, the haiku of journalism. Write every day, or almost every day, even if only a few lines, not only to keep in fighting trim but because the results may be worth perpetuating. The quality of the writing may vary inversely with the amount of time expended.

Write in forms, whether traditional or ad hoc. The sestina form was once exotic. Now, after masterly examples by Auden, Bishop, Ashbery, Anthony Hecht, Donald Justice, Harry Mathews, James Cummins, it sometimes seems as if the sestina is that restaurant Yogi Berra had in mind when he said, "No one eats there any more—it's too crowded." I once received a rejection slip from John Frederick Nims, then the editor of "Poetry" magazine, saying that he was returning a sestina I had sent him because "sestinas are a dime a dozen." In fact, however, poets continue to write sestinas that are amazingly fresh and inventive. After a stimulating gossip session with Jim Cummins, who had set a precedent by writing a sestina using "Gary Snyder" as one of his six recurring end-words, I wrote "Sestina," choosing as end words the names of poets (Walt Whitman, Ted Berrigan, Anne Sexton, Marvin Bell, Philip Levine, and a variable). The poem was written with malice toward no one. I had just happened to read an interview with Ted Berrigan in which he was asked to state his opinion of Rod McKuen. He said something like, "I don't mind McKuen, I begrudge no man his right to make a living. My idea of a bad poet is Marvin Bell." This seemed an extraordinary statement, implying that competent mediocrity was more of a sin than true badness. So, I put it into the sestina as part of the mix, without prejudice.

Comedy, wit, humor, satire, japes and jibes—all are valid. The comic or ironic impulse can heighten the tragic—in *Hamlet* and *King Lear*, for instance. When I was a freshman in college, I wrote a paper on the funny parts of *Paradise Lost*. This was considered a brash and eccentric thing to do, as *Paradise Lost* is thought not to have any funny parts. (I quoted lines from Book IV that were, I argued, beautiful but slightly ridiculous: "the unwieldy elephant, / To make them mirth, used all his might, and wreathed / His lithe proboscis.") The comic is underrated and complicated. Comedy affirms, but comedy can also express (or cunningly conceal) savage indignation. Wit as a term encompasses not only clever word play, skill at repartee, a flair for a turn of phrase, but also a way the intelligence has of apprehending the world.

When I resumed teaching poetry writing in the mid-1990s after many years of not doing it, I noticed that students were writing poems based on experience, so I devised assignments to emphasize the possibility that poetry could be linguistically generated, that you could arrive at truth or beauty or both without being fully aware of what you were up to. In fact, the conscious mind may get in the way. Therefore, it is useful to occupy the conscious mind with something it can profitably do, like solve a word puzzle. Sometimes writing a poem is as much about solving a problem or puzzle as it is about resolving a crisis. A poem is the consequence of a game played with invisible cards and dice.

When I teach, I enjoy distributing a poem in a language foreign to the students and asking them to translate it without the help of a dictionary. The mistranslation assignment invariably generates interesting work. I like doing the same assignments I give to students. In 1997 I asked my students at the New School to write a poem or prose poem in a form adapted from a public mode of discourse not usually associated with poetry, like a menu or recipe. When I did the assignment, I chose the errors column in the *New York Times* as my model. It appeared in *Harper's* under the title "Mistakes Were Made."

Another assignment I like giving myself and others is to write a poem that does the work of an obituary. "A shilling life will give you all the facts," Auden wrote about a certain type of biography. I wanted to give not all the facts but some striking ones, and some fancies too, in such a biographical poem as "Wittgenstein's Ladder."

The poet's chief obligation is to keep poetry alive. Poetry, if genuine, is a resistance manifested against what would conspire against it. Wallace Stevens has the phrase "the pressure of reality" in one of his essays. He talks about the imagination pressing back against this pressure. The best way to manifest resistance is not by writing a poem that narrowly protests a particular injustice, but by writing a poem that on the surface has no bearing on that injustice, a poem that renews the possibility of human imagination in a sphere where that is endangered.

At the University of Cincinnati, where I taught as the Elliston Poet in Residence, I was asked what advice I would give to young writers. I looked at the bright, eager faces in the room, and I said—I didn't know I was going to say this, it was just what I felt at that moment—that they should remember that poetry is not life. That there will come a time when all of them will feel envy and resentment, because they didn't get the job they deserved, or the award, or the recognition. There is no one is the poetry world who feels he or she has received the recognition they deserve. The question is: How will you deal with the bitterness and resentment? Because those things are the enemies of poetry. Those things are not real not real in the sense that grief and love are real. Unfortunately, it's all too easy to succumb to competitive envy. And that is why it is important to remember that poetry is not the whole of one's life, but a part of it, and that we should not put too great a burden on the poetry that we love. Keeping it alive, poetry and the possibility of poetry, is the great thing.

VI. LETTERS TO YOUNG POETS

Dear Karl. I'm glad your reading list includes the mother of all lofty letters to young writers, Rilke's: "There is only one way. You have to go into yourself. Determine why you write. Has the source spread its roots in the depths of your heart? Ask yourself whether you would have to die if you couldn't write. This above all—ask yourself in the stillness of the night: must I write?" Yes, read *Letters to a Young Poet*; his elegies and sonnets, too. But don't stop there. Read Keats's letters, Emerson's essays,

Gertrude Stein's lectures, Randall Jarrell's criticism, Auden's prose. Read everything and everyone and imitate someone great. The best exercise is to imitate something great. Next best is to write in forms.

Dear Allyson. I loved what you said about resisting the impulse to write a motherlove poem and think, "There, that's perfect, that's lovely."

Dear Danielle. I agree. Adding "you" to an "I" poem almost always improves it. There are other tenses besides the present, other points of view besides the first person singular, other things to write about besides the errands of the day and the horrors of war.

Dear Carly. The enemy of poetry is *should*.

Dear Peter. James Merrill in an interview warned against the tendency to rely on "the first-person present active indicative." The present tense is, Merrill said, a "hot" tense that "can't be handled for very long without cool pasts and futures to temper it; or some complexity of syntax, or a modulation into the conditional—some alternative relation to experience. Otherwise, you get this addictive, self-centered immediacy, harder to break oneself out of than cigarettes."

Dear Mark, Mia, Patrick, Huy, Shobita, Matthew, Erin, John, and Alex. You can rescue an unsatisfactory poem by wrecking it. You wreck it by scrambling the lines or running them backward, omitting every second word, or replacing every noun with, say, "Ohio."

Dear Loretta, Christine and Anita. Feel free to dislike anything. As James Schuyler put it: "Ulysses" is a masterpiece "I suppose," but "freedom of choice is better."

Dear Chris. Hello. Sometimes it is easier to write love poems when you are not in love. A love poem does not have to be written to anyone in particular. A love poem invents its recipient. P. said: The reader comes into existence when the writer ceases to be. Not sure I agree with that. O. said: Sincerity is a bogus virtue in poetry. You don't respond to Shakespeare's sonnets by testing their sincerity. E. said: the less autobiographical, the truer the poem. If you write "my father," the reader will assume

you're writing about your father even when you aren't. So be it. The last
sentences of Samuel Beckett's *Molloy* describe the universal origin of all
writing: "Then I went back into the house and wrote, It is midnight. The
rain is beating on the windows. It was not midnight. It was not raining."

Dear Anne and Mark. Don't feel you need to make sense all the time. Your
poems don't have to change the world. They just have to give pleasure.

Dear Ruth. Good revision. The ending is lovely, as is the personification
of the car ("hot yellow eyes") and the streak of monosyllables in line five.
Cut "the crunch of leaves underfoot."

Dear Len. You might want to give William Blake's "Songs of Innocence"
a second chance. Don't worry about the tenpage paper due in December.
You have already fulfilled the requirement.

Dear Sarah, Rebecca, and Rachel. Do not read reviews. Many people with
strong opinions and the need to air them are loudmouths or bullies, and if
you could see them for what they are, you wouldn't crave their approval.

Dear Victor. Ignore the asshole. Isn't it amazing that the very people who
take pride in voicing obnoxious or offensive statements so often turn out
to have such thin skins?

Dear Nikki. Writing about what you know may not be as great as writing
about what you don't (yet) know, but it sure beats writing about the dia-
lectics of loss, bullshit without a dream, gnostic visions of critical theory
as the latest capitalist rip-off plot, ambition without heart, energy without mind, or the satisfactions of the flatterer, who masturbates in hell
writing self-aware narratives.

Dear Laura, Megin, Justin, Matthew, Erin, and Phoebe. Eight drops
cedarwood oil, two cups sea salt, two cups baking soda. Soak for twenty
minutes.

Dear friends. There will come a time when someone else will win the
prize you wanted, the job you coveted, or the publication you were bank-
ing on. It might even be the person sitting next to you right now. And you

will feel envy, you will feel resentment—you wouldn't be human if you didn't. But you cannot afford to give in to these feelings, which are poison to a writer. To ward them off, you will need to go deeper into yourself, into your heart. You will need to remember that awards and publications and jobs—great as they are to achieve—are not the reason you undertook to do this work in the first place.

Dear Victoria. Pity the spiteful. They communicate their disappointment in life.

Dear Shanna. Hello. It is one fifty a.m., and no one is sleeping.

Denise Low

The Womanly Lineage of Writerly Mentors

SHE WAS AMONG THE FIRST WAVE of feminists in the early 1960s as she asserted her place in a male-dominated profession. Instead of playing bridge at the country club with the other wives of lawyers, Marjorie Sullivan went to graduate school and became a professor in the local college. She had raised two children, found an academic position, and now she also took time to mentor me, in addition to her work tasks.

I was sixteen, the last child of a railroad worker, of mixed Native and British Isles heritage, and deeply depressed. I was bookish. We entered into an informal contract of literary relationship of mentor and follower, a family-like structure not yet diagrammed by sociologists.

Mrs. Sullivan—I would never use her first name—first helped me with poems when she was ending a stint of teaching high school English. In her classroom she stood amidst orderly rows of desks. She was highly manicured, with a coif of tightly curled reddish-blonde hair. A high forehead dominated her face, and below it her icy blue eyes shined. She wore proper pearls with her tailored suit. She was the opposite of my own mother, whose wispy hair never showed any kind of order.

Mrs. Sullivan's suit reminded me that we once had crossed paths at the local Congregational Church. One Easter my mother had sewn me an unfashionable but fine jacket, of houndstooth wool, which I wore reluctantly. Mrs. Sullivan stopped me in the crowded vestibule hallway and noticed the expertly sewn garment. "Did your mother make this?" she asked, as she fingered the perfect pucker at the shoulder seam. I nodded, surprised. "It's beautifully made," she said and walked away. Her interest in the well-crafted jacket comes back to me as characteristic of her interest in finely wrought objects, whatever the medium.

In our first meeting at the high school, she agreed to look at poem drafts if I would read other poets. I was disappointed. Even as a youngster, I wanted someone to proclaim my work spectacular. Approval was my goal more than developing skill. Now that I have some accomplishments in the writer's universe, and especially as a state poet laureate, writers of all ilk have engaged with me for exactly the same purpose. I understand all too well. Reluctantly, I submitted to Mrs. Sullivan's suggestions and was the better for it, as my solipsism and depression slowly lifted. We began irregular meetings that would last twenty years.

The summer before my senior year in high school was especially important. Every couple of weeks, I walked to Mrs. Sullivan's house. Rather than dismember my poems, she scanned them politely and suggested corrective readings. We read Albert Camus's *The Stranger*, which introduced the idea of an indifferent universe. This concept of randomness was an antidote to my self-pity. Next was *The Plague*, set in a locked-down town that echoed my own sense of imprisonment in our isolated Kansas domicile. Looking back, I can see that my mentor was augmenting my ability to place characters in historic contexts. French existentialists speak to the situation of land-locked United States citizens in the aftermath of the American Indian Wars of the Great Plains. These wars, had ended just a generation before Mrs. Sullivan's birth, and I was the next generation. She chose books strategically.

During that hot summer poetry appeared in my journal in its own stream of meandering lines. I can remember only one poem in any detail: an attempt at absurdism with a metaphor about orange slices exchanged for slats in a shopping cart. I had read Allen Ginsberg's poem "A Supermarket in California" and was inspired, although I was not yet an effective crafter of words.

Mrs. Sullivan loved the Latin American writers, especially those of the surrealist strain. She impressed upon me how far advanced in their ideas of human consciousness were Carlos Fuentes, Julio Cortázar, Jorge Luis Borges, and Gabriel García Márquez. She celebrated their connections to Indigenous cultures, perhaps as a way to help me connect my own mismatched heritages. She loved the inventions of magical surrealism. This was radical in the mid-1960s, a peak time of the British literary canon.

In her artfully composed living room, Mrs. Sullivan talked about recent Cuban immigrants, refugees from Castro, who filled her college classes. The Cubans had been driven away from their homes through the upheavals of revolution. Like Camus, she imparted no judgement. She took them to local theatrical plays and concerts. To me she stressed her role as a bridge between cultures. "They need someone to help explain the noisy cicadas," she said one day. She smiled and added, "How do you begin to explain William L. White?" This son of the famous journalist William Allen White was the bête noire of the town. I laughed with her at this insider joke.

An abstract painting of a jazz trio stretched over the wall opposite the couch where I sat, and it influenced me as much as the informal lectures. Its lines did not exactly meet, but rather suggested forms. I learned a lot from that visual prompt, as well from Mrs. Sullivan's library, about how to live my odd-shaped life with many blanks to fill in.

As that summer drew to a close, and my departure for college neared, the huddles in Mrs. Sullivan's living room became even sweeter. A great unknown space lay before me, but cherished books from my mentor's tutelage would accompany me into that future. I tried to keep up with her recommendations: Truman Capote's *In Cold Blood*, with a few scenes filmed in our town. Saul Bellow's *Herzog*. Joan Didion's *Run River*.

Those last months, my mother allowed me to take over the kitchen and experiment with baking. One success was a cinnamon-and nutmeg apple bread. In an inspired moment, I thought to take a gift of bread to my mentor. I loaded the last of the borrowed books into a grocery sack and laid a loaf of the warm bread on top. This was the first time I considered her perspective, how she had found time to talk with me despite her duties as wife, mother, and professor. Teachers are hired to instruct, but mentors choose to take on that apprenticeship with no remuneration nor other tangible reward.

I climbed the stairs to her split-level doorstep, knocked, waited, and no answer. I almost had descended when she opened the door and found the fragrant apple bread. Her face lit up. That was worth everything. We were not demonstrative people, and it was years before hugging became an accepted practice in Kansas. That moment, however understated, was when I learned the glow of reciprocation. On that faraway porch and in a small way, I learned to be an adult. Indirectly, I learned to be a better writer as I learned to shift points of view from my own ego.

While I was in college, Mrs. Sullivan moved to Kansas City to a swanky assisted-care place. She simultaneously nursed her mother, who lived to be a hundred, and her disabled husband. At my first visit, when my children were darling toddlers, she explained women's life cycles, how women spend more time caring for aged relatives than rearing their children. She was right, as I learned with my own parents.

In the city, in between caretaking, she thrived. She had access to art galleries, drama, and a symphony. I visited every so often and enjoyed the same abstract jazz painting from her former living room. We went to art galleries and dined at an art museum's Italianate restaurant. We discussed women's work, writing, and books. She loved fantasies of Italo Calvino like *Invisible Cities*, with its allegories that invoked the Great Chain of Being and subverted it. We talked through its layers. She liked Umberto Eco's *The Name of the Rose* and encouraged me to savor its details.

In time, she moved to be near her grown son in another state. The last time I saw her, I treated her to high tea at a fancy hotel, which she relished. We discussed Gore Vidal's *Lincoln*, with its blend of factual and imagined history. She emphasized again the importance of Fuentes. When we parted I was too young, even in my thirties, to understand how much I was losing. We corresponded intermittently until she died in 2006, at ninety-two.

Mrs. Sullivan shared a cosmopolitan approach to literature as she led me through works of master writers. She understood the challenges I would face as a woman writer and professor. She had two sons and no daughter, so I imagine I reciprocated her generosity in the simple fact of my gender. In turn, I have become a mentor and a teacher of many students, and I continue her teachings in my own fashion. A living river of relationships parallels the literature of written texts, equally as rich. Mrs. Sullivan chose to invest herself in a lonely teenager with few prospects. I am so grateful.

Sandy McIntosh

Writing Influences — "Why Should I Write Another Book?"

WE WERE TABLE PARTNERS at the Elaine Benson Gallery in Bridgehampton, at the annual Steinbeck "Meet the Writers" book signing.

"I've had three or four good ideas for books, and I've written them all," Joseph Heller said.

Indeed, they were good ideas. I had read his first and most famous novel, *Catch-22*, six times straight through lying on my military school bunk, each time basking in my personal realizations sparked by that book—that the demented, twisted quasi-military reality I'd endured for six years was, in fact, entirely absurd, and that Heller had articulated the absurdity.

I had read his novels that followed: *Something Happened, Good as Gold*, the play *We Bombed in New Haven*, and others. "But I think I liked *Picture This* best of all," I told him as in that moment, I had just realized it.

"That's because it is a book about an idea. It is the idea that is the lead character."

The story navigates history, from ancient Athens through Holland in the seventeenth century, to the founding of the American empire, all connected by Rembrandt's painting *Aristotle Contemplating a Bust of Homer*.

"It's the painting itself. People take it as satire. I didn't write it that way."

I recalled the reviews I had read which panned the book, though I never doubted the book's greatness. I told Heller that.

"Ah," he said.

I was a younger writer, and a hero-worshipping fan, and he had a reputation for being arch with young aspirants. But he turned to appraise me for the first time. He seemed gratified that I had intuited his novel's deeper intentions.

Our conversation was interrupted frequently as people lined up to ask Heller to sign copies of his books, especially *Catch-22*, stacked on the table between us. (Of course, I had copies of my own book, *Firing Back*, a business how-to that few among that literary crowd in attendance were interested in having me sign.)

At some point, my fiancé, Barbara, came up to the table with a plastic cup of red wine for me, the kind of cheap-yet-drinkable wine ever-present at literary events. At the same time, Heller's wife, Valerie, brought him Scotch in a cut crystal glass. Looking at his glass and indicating my own I asked him, "Does this mean you get special treatment around here?" He answered, "Of course. Why shouldn't I?"

A young woman stepped up and told him how much she had loved his autobiographical *Then and Now*, about growing up in Coney Island and his time in the Army Air Corp. She pointed to the photograph of the twenty-year-old Heller on the cover. "You were so handsome back then."

"What do you mean 'back then'? I'm damn handsome now," he said.

Barbara wanted to be introduced and I told Heller that we were going to be married the next day in East Hampton. He smiled and drew from his wallet a one-dollar bill. "Mazel tov," he said. Barbara asked him to sign the bill. I said he should sign it "Irving Washington," which was an absurd name from *Catch-22*, typical of Heller's humor, in which he put a spin on the revered WASP name of a person by making it into something homey and Yiddish. But he would not do as I asked, instead signing his real name. "You'll find this more valuable," he said.

Eventually, all the books that Heller had brought were signed. His many fans were disappointed, but I had an idea. Why not get him to sign copies of my book? That seemed the only way for me to move a few copies with that audience.

He said no. I argued that he could write something in my book such as "Not by Joseph Heller." He seemed to waver when I told him it was the only way to sell my books. But then turned me down. "What's in it for me?" he said.

I raised the question again of a new book, and why he should write it. "You have people waiting for a new Joseph Heller," I told him.

"Yes. So, I should write a book because people demand it?" Then he hesitated. "Well," he said," I am working on something. I can't say what it is, whether it's even a good idea. And maybe I'm writing it only because people want me to write it."

One year later, at the Steinbeck "Meet the Writers," Heller and I were back, but not tablemates this time. "I don't know if you remember me," I said when I reached the front of his autograph line.

"Of course, I do," he said. "And I wrote a new book like I promised. It will be out next year."

It was *Portrait of the Artist as an Old Man.*

"It's an experiment. I took ideas I'd had for stories and novels and wove them together. They're all connected, I think. I've got a section in it called 'The Sexual Biography of My Wife'. I'm not sure whether she's comfortable with that," he said. "But at least I had fun reading it to her." He paused. "No," he continued as if answering a question I had not asked. "It wasn't a vanity project."

The novel depicts an aging author, Eugene Pota, a prominent writer trying to produce a novel from bits and pieces that is as successful as his earlier work. He knows it is his last large piece of fiction and hopes against hope it is a magnum opus. It was published posthumously in 2000. It is not a major work. Its loose parts of beginnings and endings have little energy of the familiar, Heller kind. At its end, we leave the narrator at a loss, the unknotted fabric of a longer story in his hands. Was it only a book written to satisfy his fans, readers like me?

I think about Charles Ives, how one day he came to his wife, tears in his eyes, to tell her that he could no long compose music. The notes didn't align, the sounds were hollow. And from then on, he set himself to revise old projects. He got on with his insurance business.

Is there an end to one's imagination? Is it a cul-de-sac, a joyless wrong turning, or is it a natural ending in the sand? *You may come this far, but no farther; here your proud waves must stop.*

Jane Hirshfield

A Continuously Accidental and Precarious Thing

Interview with Mary Mackey

Did you read poetry as a child? What was your first significant encounter with poetry?

The first book I bought with my own allowance money, at age seven or eight, was a book of Japanese haiku, discovered on one of those metal spiral display stands in a stationary store on First Avenue in the East 20s. I have no idea now what a child growing up in New York City found in these poems, whose vocabulary of meaning-making was falling blossoms I'd never known, singing birds I'd never heard, darkness and moonlight I'd seen only by peering past streetlights. The more I've since learned about haiku, the more I've come to realize how complex their registries of feeling and thought are. I can't have grasped any of that as a child. But I suspect that I recognized in those poems a world I wanted to live in—a world whose windows opened to a larger existence.

A few years later, I was entirely transfixed by Walter de la Mare's "The Listeners." My childhood home was a place of blunt, literal, and unnuanced speech; of discomfort with the unknown and dismay at the unplanned for. That poem offers a different way of being. It enacts the power and depth and beauty of unanswered questions, unresolved situations. In it, silence is not mere abyss. Its rich paradox is to propose unseen presences receiving even our unanswered callings. Most of my callings back then were both unuttered and answered; the poem promised that this was not how it must always be. There's also de la Mare's irresistible music. In the fifth-grade poetry anthology, which I still own, written next to the phrase "the forest's ferny floor" in round, careful script is the word "alliteration."

Do you have any degrees or formal education in creative writing?

As an undergraduate I designed my own major, "Creative Writing and Literature in Translation." That doesn't mean I was translating; it meant that instead of reading English literature I was reading works in languages I didn't know, to which the professors could give me some better entrance: Greek Tragedy in Translation, Chinese Poetry in Translation, Japanese Noh Drama. I never went to graduate school. I did take, for three years, an adult-ed night course offered through U.C. Berkeley. Every other week, some major visiting poet would visit, and so I learned the vocabulary of craft from Galway Kinnell, Margaret Atwood, Robert Bly, Carolyn Forche, Robert Pinsky, Carolyn Kizer, Robert Hass, Philip Levine, William Matthews . . . what luck. There are many paths to an education, and the most important of all is simply reading, as widely as possible, with voracious awareness. But having some craft vocabulary increases the possibilities of awareness.

When did you write your first poem and what prompted you to write it?

Of this I have no recollection. All I can say is that by the time I had learned to write at all, I set down on one of those large brown pieces of paper with blue wide lines on them: "I want to be a writer when I grow up." I would not have remembered that either, but my mother saved it and gave it to me after my first, small press book came out, when I was twenty-nine. I have no gift for narrative or dialogue, and so it was always poems I wrote when I wrote for myself. I hid them under the mattress, somehow believing my mother wouldn't have found them. That sense of privacy was deeply important—for me, writing wasn't a performance for others, it was the construction of a self by what felt a secret life-raft.

What are your sources of inspiration?

I can't predict inspiration ahead of time. It might be a life event—all the arrivals, departures, precipices, and pinnacles that any life brings will carry their poems. It might be a question. It might be a newspaper article—every book I've published includes work that looks at the wars that seem never to end. One poem is about the genocide in Rwanda, another was precipitated by the Supreme Court nomination of Robert Bork. (That one was stopped.) Poems have been awakened by a chair left outside in winter, by a small hole on the side of a path I was daily running past, by a *New York Times* Tuesday Science article about discovering the workings of itch. Abstract ideas can suddenly become pressing. I've written about my ambivalent relationship to judgment and to opinion, I've written about the conjunction "and" and the preposition "to." Increasingly, poems have been summoned into being by the crises of the biosphere—climate change, species' vanishing—and of social justice.

There's what might get a poem started, and where it may end. Poems are "about" what precipitates them, but then also are about whatever of larger meaning constellates around that starting-out place, changes and expands it. In poems, the unsayable haunts whatever is able to be said. Something throws a person off-balance. The poem is the work of the feet, hurrying to catch you before you fall. When you look up again, it's into a different world.

What poets do you admire?

I have always a terrible time answering this question. The list is too long and varied. I am promiscuous in my poetry loves.

Did you decide to become a poet or did it just happen?

I'm not sure I could distinguish between these two. I wrote a poem. Then I wrote another. Then another. Eventually I showed them to friends. People send things to magazines, so I did. People make books, so I did. I did do all these things, from the outside it must all look very intentional, yet my life in poetry feels to me a continually accidental and precarious thing. It is nothing I count on. Perhaps tomorrow I may no longer be a poet. It depends on the next poem coming when I've lost balance, and that is something I am never entirely sure will happen.

What obstacles stood in your way?

A poem that will be in my next book says: "Whatever distances the heart,

I have brought here. / Whatever handcuffs the soul, I have brought here." If the outer world has sent obstacles, that would be to the 'career,' perhaps—but not to the writing. The writing is my own to do, or not do. And so, I must answer: distraction, depression, fear, the exigencies of other demands and other kinds of work, lassitude, the life-bludgeons that have brought me at times to silence. Even my own comfort with silence may be something that's stood in my way. I'm entirely happy to read poems by others. I'm happy to spend time in an unlanguaged world. But really, how many poems can one person write? Even for the most prolific poet, 1000 or so in a lifetime. And of those, how many that matter? A handful. The rest may be interesting, may be necessary, but it's the handful that matter. As Randall Jarrell put it, a poet spends a lifetime standing out in thunderstorms hoping to be hit a half dozen times by lightning.

What or who helped you?

The lifelong desire to want more than I could find except through the search-instrument of deepened language. A community of friends—fellow writers, research scientists, carpenters, artists, cooks.... And even though I wrote first to make my own way in private, it later helped that people I did not know seemed to want my poems. My third published poem was taken by *The New Yorker*, in 1982, when Howard Moss was the editor. No one says such an august editor will take a poem by an entirely unknown young person, but he did. An implausibly early Guggenheim fellowship left me with a strong sense of wanting to become worthy of that gift. It helps when someone tells me that a poem I've written has been of use, a rope and piton for the steep-pitch places. I would still write if no one read my poems, I'm quite sure. But it helps, knowing my poems sometimes matter to others.

And the art itself has helped me, all the poets who became my direct and indirect influences. I learned from the compressive image-speaking of early Japanese and Chinese poetry, from the astringent awareness of certain Eastern European and Scandinavian poets of the mid-20th century, from the freedom of the South American Spanish and Portuguese poets. I learned from Adrienne Rich, from Horace and Catullus, from Szymborska and Milosz. None of us invents language, none of us invents metaphor, story, mountains, cities, the forces of gravity, grief, love. We each are this moment's sum of the world's ceaseless additions, inventions, and hungers. We are taught, by the living and by the dead, what it looks like to be a full human being. Writing poems gives me a way to make my life larger. I learned this because others' poems have made my life larger.

How did you find your poetic voice?

Sentence by sentence. My earliest book (happily unfindable) carries a little too much of the scent of the '70s in some of the poems. After that I began to write more with the voice I hear when listening with my own ears to my own tongue. At some point, early on, I realized I wanted my poems to be stranger, even at the risk of not being as "good." That desire was a liberation of voice as well.

What is the single most important thing for a young poet to know about writing poetry?

Today's answer, since tomorrow's would surely be different: Write the poem that only you could have written.

Trust your experience of the world, of your own life, of the poem. Trust that the world matters, that your life matters, that your words matter. Then doubt all these things enough to ask if what you've written is sufficient, surprising, contains art's mysterious surplus. Has the poem found something that it, and you, did not know before it was written? Have you found fully and accurately the images, the phrases, the story, the feeling, the arc and surge of transformation? Then trust again, because if you only doubt, you will overwork the dough until no living yeast remains in it; if you over-doubt, you will try to please others instead of your own sense of the poem, of your life, of the world. Be willing for your work to be odd, peculiar, to be itself in the way a giraffe is itself and knows no other shape or gait of being. By such strange inventions of existence, the poem becomes the poem, the world becomes the world, a person becomes, perhaps, a more fully human person.

Jason McCall

Who Are You?

IF I SAY I STARTED WRITING to find myself, then I'm only telling a half truth. Growing up, I had a clear identity. I knew who I was because of all the teachers, church members, and relatives who reminded me of who I was. I was Lindsey's brother. And Shonda's brother. And Tonya's Brother. And Ethel's boy. And Lindsey's boy. I am the baby of my family. It's fun to tell that to my young nieces and nephew and see them try to sort out how a grown man can still be a baby. But it wasn't always a source of fun with me. Like the youngest member of many families, growing up, my existence was normally explained by a point of reference. When I was smart, I was smart just like my brother and sisters. When my dad got me a job working at the hotel where he worked as a chef for his second job, the managers told me I laughed just like my dad. When I open my eyes, my wife tells me I have my mother's eyes.

And like the youngest member of many families, I hated the constant comparison to my family members. Most of the comparisons were related to my brother because we were only four years apart. He cheered for the Giants during Super Bowl XXV, so I cheered for the Buffalo Bills. When we played *Mortal Kombat*, he liked Sub-Zero, so I played as Sub-Zero's rival Scorpion. When he went to the gifted high school and began to talk about a future in science and math, I knew I didn't want a future in science and math.

The only problem was that I was good at science and math. I was smart because I got to spend my childhood in a house filled with smart people. Even now, after my success as a writer and teacher, I still have no problem admitting that my smarts were nothing special in my household. My parents knew I was smart, too, so they decided I had to spend junior high and high school at gifted schools, too.

I walked through junior high school grumbling to myself about how I didn't want to be there. The school was a world away from my neighborhood. I was one of the only black faces in every classroom, and on top of being awkward teenagers, most of the students were awkward teenagers who didn't know what to do when an awkward black teenager sat next to them. Coming of age in that environment was invaluable. I learned how to make small talk with people I had very little to nothing in common with, and I started to learn how to define myself in a new crowd.

I made my share of friends. I tried to remember to smiled back at the pretty girls who smiled at me. I tried to make sure that I represented during basketball games in the gym and during games of Trivial Pursuit in Latin class. I have to admit that my Latin class trivial pursuit skills were far beyond my basketball skills. On the basketball court, I could jump and touch the rim with two hands, but I couldn't dunk. I dunked on all of the opposing teams when I played Latin class Trivial Pursuit.

My junior high memories consist of a lot of Latin class, a lot of lonely moments in the lunchroom, and most importantly, my decision one day to not pay attention in my 8th grade history class.

I'm pretty sure it was an Alabama or American History class, and that was part of my motivation to take days off in class. I love the ancient stuff, but I start to drift and doze once Western history makes it to the 95 Theses and Jamestown and Papal Bulls. I was good at remembering dates and I was good at knowing how to connect the dots between those dates, so I could succeed in most history classes without bringing much of myself into the room. One day, while I was going through the motions of being a history student, I noticed a sign-up sheet for a creative writing elective class.

I never thought about being a writer before this point. Even today, I really don't think about *being* a writer; writing still feels like a loved hobby more than a calling or quest or vocation. But I saw that sign-up sheet for the creative writing elective class, and I saw a way out for me.

As my 8th grade year progressed, my parents began to talk to me about high school and their expectations for my high school. In Alabama at the time, most junior high schools stopped at 9th grade, and most high schools started at 10th grade. My parents started to ask about how I would feel going to the same gifted high school my brother and oldest sister attended. I knew that, without another gifted school as an alternative, these questions were mostly acts of parental kindness. During conversations about school, my mother would always talk about how I needed to be challenged just like my sisters and brother needed to be challenged.

Just like my sisters and brother.

I didn't know how to write, and I didn't know if I would like writing, but I knew that I never heard my sisters or my brother talk about taking a creative writing class. Taking creative writing meant giving up my computer programming elective, and that might have been the hardest part of the decision. I was good enough at junior high computer programming. I could write enough code to make a ball bounce around the screen as a screensaver. I could make blatant *Jeopardy* rip-off. My proudest computer moment came from a rudimentary battle arena game that I made that allowed players to pick their own weapons and armors. I was good enough at computer programming, but I never really loved it. And my brother liked computers, too. Leaving computer class was another way to leave him. Also, I knew that there was a gifted school in the city that focused on arts instead of strictly academics. Before I even thought about writing my first poems or short stories, I saw the creative writing class as a way to find myself, as a space where I wouldn't have to fight through all the shadows my family casts.

The 9th grade creative class led me to the gifted high school for the arts. The gifted high school for the arts led me to minor in creative writing in college. The minor in creative writing led to a Master of Fine Arts degree in creative writing. The Master of Fine Arts degree led me to the classroom and led me to my current relationship with words and the page.

Who are you?

Homer will always be my favorite author, and the question of identity lingers in both of his epic poems. The Greek and Trojan heroes often take time to introduce themselves and give their lineage before doing battle. One of my favorite scenes of *The Iliad* is the scene in book VI when Diomedes and Glaucus meet to do battle but instead end up exchanging gifts once they realize their grandfathers were friends. The question of identity also echoes in the cyclops Polyphemus' cave in when Odysseus and his men are trapped there in *The Odyssey*. Odysseus uses his wit to claim his name is No Man, and when he manages to escape the cave by stabbing Polyphemus in the eye, Polyphemus' claims that No Man is attacking him go unanswered by his cyclops brethren because if he is being attacked by "No Man," then his attacker must be a god. Odysseus shows his identity not by his name, but by his actions. Odysseus only gives his true name after he believes that he and his men have safely escaped and made it back to their ships. However, Polyphemus uses Odysseus' name to curse the hero's journey back to Ithaca.

Odysseus is not his name; Odysseus is his actions. Odysseus is the Trojan Horse. Odysseus is the disguise he swears to sneak back into his home to reclaim his wife and kingdom. Odysseus is the nighttime raids with Diomedes to steal the Palladium and the horses of king Rhesus. The first name Odysseus gives to Polyphemus is truer than the second name he gives as he is sailing away because the first name shows Odysseus for what he truly is: a trickster, a con, a fraud.

Who are you?

As writers, we do not get to play the role of a Greek legend often, but this question is at least as hard for writers as it is for legendary heroes. Usually, after I introduce myself as a writer, the next question is "What do you write about?" "What do you write about?" is another way of asking "Who are you?" As writers, our work is part of our identity, and our identity, fair or not, is expected to be part of our work. When I get questions about what I write, I normally give a bloated answer about how I'm a lyric poet who focuses on narrative and tradition. I talk about how my love of origin stories drove me to writing. I get nods and raised eyebrows when I compare different versions of superheroes to different versions of gods and heroes in the Greco-Roman world. I get a few laughs when I talk about how many dead wrestlers and Trojan War epithets I can fit into one poem.

My answers usually satisfy the person asking. Many people are impressed by someone who writes poetry because many still people see poetry as *poetry*, an intimate whisper of longing / insight / unity with the earth, or "POETRY," a mystical art that few can tap into and even fewer can understand. This aura around poetry exists despite the fact that there are more avenues than ever to become involved with poetry.

My most common dream is a dream where I can fly, and, honestly, I think some people would give me the same look that they give when I tell them that I am poet if I told them that I could fly. My choice to be a poet and my subject matter are usually enough to make people believe I'm somewhere between smart enough and smarter than I really am. But my answers aren't completely honest. They aren't honest at all, really.

Hidden behind the Trojan War metaphors and comic book allusions is a secret. I'm not that deep. I'm a two-trick pony who's manage to ride those two tricks to awards, publications, and some level of job security.

I remember the first two poems I ever wrote in my 9th grade creative writing class. My first poem, naturally, was a love poem about a girl I fell in love with because she was nice to me at the bus stop. My second poem was a poem about how I hated myself because I wasn't living up to my potential in the same way that Aeneas wasn't living up to his potential when he lingered in Carthage with Dido. Maybe I didn't get the girl in 9th grade because she didn't get my Aeneas references. Or my Gundam references. Or my NWO references. Or maybe I didn't get the girl in 9th grade because she had good judgment.

Regardless, my first poem and my second poem established my poetic subject matter for the next 20 years. I only write poems about two things. I write poems about the things I love, and I write poems about hating myself.

Organizing my first book made me notice my subject matter habits and limitations. My first book started as my graduate school thesis. I finished graduate school a decade after that first creative writing class. In some ways, it's a typical first book from a poet fresh out of a graduate creative writing program. It's largely autobiographical. It has three sections. There are poems in the book that read more like class exercises than poems because there are poems in the book that started as class exercises. But there's ambition in the book, too. I fought to fit all of my interests and obsessions in between the front and back cover of that book. I fought to fit pro wrestling, mythology, and my struggles with mental and emotional well being into a sixty-page narrative. I fought with writing about my family and friends and the grudges I still hold for my family and friends. But, underneath all of that and the pressure to publish a book, the book is made up of two types of poems: love poems and self-hate poems.

My two types of poems are the two tritest poems. Helen of Troy told the world everything there is to know about love and hate. Radio Raheem told the world everything there is to know about love and hate. Saying that I write about love and hate could be an admission that I should not be writing at all. Saying that I write about love and hate could be an admission that I never learned much of anything during my 20 years as a writer. There's the old writing maxim that says "Make it new." Love is not new. Hate is not new. And I do not imagine that anything I have to say about love and hate is new.

However, when I talk to other writers about poetry and my attraction to poetry, I often mention that my attraction to poetry is not its ability to make things new, but its ability to make things uncomfortable, to move things away from their expected center, to dig underneath the visible and find the forgotten. I started writing poetry to find myself, and this fight for discovery makes me think of Heinrich Schliemann, the amateur archaeologist who found the ruins of ancient Troy by retracing the steps of the old myths and legends. He was more of a fan of antiquity than a scholar, so he ruined plenty of priceless artifacts during his dig. Many experts say his dig might have ruined the remains of Homer's Troy. But Schliemann found the city, and he found treasure even it was two centuries older than Priam's treasure. For years, the history lover in me held a grudge against Schliemann for destroying what might have been the city of Priam and Hector and Paris. As a kid, I would daydream about visiting the site of Troy and kicking rocks that might have been the last remnant of the giant stone that Ajax threw at Hector in Book XIV. But as I get older and write more, my grudge fades because I realize every excavation is an act of failure. When I reach inside of myself to find writing material, I never pull out exactly what I'm searching for. I still haven't found the exact piece of me I was searching for when I sat down to write for the first time.

For me, this relates to my poetry because once I admitted to writing only two types of poems, the excavation had to begin. I had to discover why these subjects owned my poetry. I had to dig into the work and dig into myself. "Navel Gazing" is one of the dirtiest phrases in the world of creative writing criticism. It's an accusation of studying oneself without noticing or caring or relating to the outside world. However, I think navel gazing can be productive, and this thought takes me back to Greek legends as well. There was a belief in many ancient Greek religions that the *Omphalos* (Greek for "navel") at Delphi marked the center of the world. This belief amplified the belief that the oracle at Delphi held mystical powers and the ability to communicate with the gods. The *Omphalos* was the center, and power radiated from the center. Understanding of the world and the gods radiated from the center.

For me, investigating my center helped me figure out why I am the poet that I am and why I write about the subjects I choose to write about. For my poems about love, I am forced to question why I love the subjects of my poems. I am forced to question why I love professional wrestling when I know professional wrestling killed Chris Benoit, Eddie Guerrero, Andre the Giant, the British Bulldog, and so many other childhood heroes. I am forced to question why I love football when football is just another extension of a white supremacist and capitalist system profiting off of the destruction of bodies that are mostly black bodies and mostly poor bodies. I am forced to question why I love the women I love and why I write about the women I love when leaving those women out of my writing could have been the most loving thing to do. I am forced to question why I love Ancient European history and mythology when this history and mythology has been warped to demonize people who look like me. I am forced to realize that love is an act, and I am responsible for my actions. I am responsible for my writing.

For my poems about hating myself, I am forced to decide why I hate myself or parts of myself. And, of course, this excavation of myself is more important than any words I put on paper. But in reviewing my poetry, I discovered and I am still discovering that I do not hate myself in the same way that I hate the evils of the world. I don't hate myself in the same way that I hate rapists, racists, and liars. I hate myself in the same way that I hate watching bad basketball. Basketball is my favorite sport to watch. At its best, basketball is one of the best combinations of skill and strategy ever created. At its worst, it is beyond maddening. I hate watching bad basketball because I know how good basketball can be. I hate myself because I have always had a need to be better than I am at any moment.

This admission is not a revelation for me. This is not the place in this essay where I realize the error of my ways and promise to transform myself into something more complex. I might dream about flying a lot, but I gave up my dreams of being a butterfly or a phoenix a long time ago. Even though I started writing out of a need to become my own person and, there's no room for a grand metamorphosis in my poetry. Like many other artists, I have had periods where I swore that I would "break out of my shell" or "think outside of the box" and develop a new voice and touch on new subjects. Those attempts always started with good intentions and always ended with bad work. And, most of the time, the work was bad and dishonest.

These misguided attempts at transformation never produced good poetry, but the attempts did produce a good lesson. They taught me that there is no need for transformation. Coming to terms with who I am does not mean that I have to change who I am. I can't change that I am Lindsey's brother, Shonda's brother, and Tonya's brother. I can't change that I am Ethel and Lindsey's son. Luckily, I've come to terms with being the baby of my family. And I've also come to terms with who I am as a poet. Coming to terms with who I am as a poet means that I have greater responsibility to my work. I cannot blame my inspirations on a muse or some other divine inspiration. My poetry is mine. I know who I am, and I have to accept the joy, struggle, doubt, anxiety, pride, love, and hate that comes with that knowledge.

Phillip Lopate

Poetic Influence: John Keats' "When I Have Fears"

IN COLLEGE, WHERE I FIRST READ this Keats sonnet, written in 1818, published in 1848, it knocked me out.

When I Have Fears

> When I have fears that I may cease to be
> Before my pen has glean'd my teeming brain,
> Before high-piled books in charact'ry,
> Hold like rich garners the full-ripen'd grain;
> When I behold, upon the night's starr'd face,
> Huge cloudy symbols of a high romance,
> And think that I may never live to trace
> Their shadows, with the magic hand of chance,
> And when I feel, fair creature of an hour,
> That I shall never look upon thee more,
> Never have relish in the faery power
> Of unreflecting love!–then on the shore
> Of the wide world I stand alone, and think
> 'Till Love and Fame to nothingness do sink.

I loved the pile-up of "when's," the way the poem coiled tighter and tighter, until finally, in the middle of line 10, it started to release its conclusion. It was essentially an argument, with various consolations or rewards rejected in turn, like doors closing one after another. Syntax, that mighty literary tool, which is responsible for possibly one-half the charm of John Ashbery poems, and which I have since followed gladly through all the twists and turns of Samuel Johnson's, Henry James', Proust's, Thomas Bernhardt's etc.—sentences had cast its spell on me.

When when when—then! But there was something more holding me to that poem. I identified with this young man's fears that he would never live long enough to achieve the promise of his writing ambition or find happiness in romantic love. And in a sense, this premonition was right: Keats did die too young, though he wrote as beautifully as any poet can. Years later, I paid my homage by visiting the rooms where he died, above the Spanish Steps in Rome.

Still later, in the current year 2021, I have managed to write a shelf-full of books which may not "hold rich garners of full-ripen'd grain," but are adequate for their purposes, and I have been married to the same woman for over thirty years. But when I read this poem the first time, I was an adolescent, filled with doubts about my capacity to write well enough or attract the affection of women. So much so that I tried to kill myself when I was seventeen—to embrace that "nothingness" that would release me from the tension of striving without a clear end in sight. It was that same nothingness that one finds traces of in Buddhism and Hinduism, and which Jehovah for Jews and Jesus for Christians barely provide an out. I was a scholarship boy from the ghetto trying to use his brains as cudgels to storm the city of success, and a part of me kept wondering: What is the point? Is it really worth it?

Love and Fame, those two goals Freud named as the driving forces of the ego, and which the suicidal Berryman chose as the ironic title of his late collection, would they come to me? Or would they sink to nothingness? I eventually reconciled myself to the job of putting forward my best effort, step by step, but I have remained enchanted by narratives that refuse redemption or transcendence, that offer only a bleak irresolution, like this poem.

Denise Duhamel

Mr. Rogers and Me

I STARTED WRITING "BOOKS" in the fourth grade while sequestered in Crawford Allen Children's Hospital in Providence, RI. A severe asthmatic, I befriended other kids with ailments who became the basis for my characters. In one such "novel," the girl with cancer has magical, witchy powers because of her chemo treatments and cast spells turning our foul-tasting medicines into apple juice. In another, the boy with cystic fibrosis has a cape and, curing all our illnesses, leads us in an escape from the hospital. My one of a kind, self-published "books" were hand written on 3-hole lined paper, tied together with ribbons to form a spine, and decorated with my own cover art. The backs spouted fake blurbs with celebrities popular in 1971: *This book changed my life!* Mary Tyler Moore. Or *possibly the best book of the century.* Mr. Rogers.

Fred Rogers was famous for saying, "Anything that's human is mentionable, and anything that is mentionable can be more manageable." (I was delighted to see that Sarah Silverman also takes this to heart, repeating Rogers' mantra often in her 2017 Hulu show "I Love You, America.") In fourth grade I had no idea contemporary poets existed or that poetry was about "saying the unsayable," a riff on Mr. Rogers' motto. I have vivid memories of the time—breathing machines that left a salt rim on my lips; ham salad sandwiches (my least favorite meal) on green plastic institutional plates; and most poignant, a boy with leukemia to whom I liked to read. He was bald, in 6th grade, and the object and subject of my affection. One of my books (in which I tried to hide my identity) was about a marriage between two kids who met in a children's hospital long ago and who, as adults, were miraculously healthy. In another one of the books I made, this boy is Sleeping Beauty and I, The Prince. Only I am able to wake him and cure him of the evil spell of his disease. When this boy died before I was released, my fate as a writer was sealed. I remember thinking that I could somehow write my way out of my despair and, for the rest of my life, I suppose I have been doing just that. I wrote about this boy on and off over the years. My first full-length book *Smile!* (1993) includes "A First-Love Poem" in which I imagine I can still rescue him.

I have little memory of writing poetry back in the hospital. I was sure I would be a novelist or a reporter or some other kind of prose writer. I had a sense that all poets were dead—that no one wrote poems anymore just as no one still made their own shoes. I had some notion of poetry, but if you had asked me back then (no one ever did) I would have answered that it was a quaint art no longer being practiced. In kindergarten, my grandmother had taken my sister and me for our first library cards. My sister, a year younger than I and by all accounts healthy, loved Dr. Seuss's *Green Eggs and Ham.* I was a sucker for *A Child's Garden of Verses*, which I repeatedly took out of the library. I had memorized Robert Louis Stevenson's "The Land of Counterpane." I remember looking up "counterpane" in the dictionary and was delighted to learn that it meant "bedspread." Still, how it spoke to me! Though Stevenson's narrator played with soldiers rather than Colorforms or coloring books (my two favorite toys), this child was clearly like me—someone who, afflicted with illness, spends his time imagining he is a giant controlling the fate of the toy soldiers on his sheets and pillows which are transformed into hills, dales, and plains. I read *Treasure Island* a few years later, but it was Stevenson's poem that haunted me.

Much of my junior high and high school life was about taking the "creative option" in lieu of papers or exams. I was decidedly a weird kid, always befriending the misfits because I was a misfit myself. In addition to my inhaler, I had a portable breathing machine and couldn't tolerate smoke or animal dander, to which I had severe allergic reactions. This limited my ability to go to school dances—everyone still smoked back then in public places—and to the houses of friends who had pets. I could only fit into "chubette" size clothes from Sears. The Sears slogan was "Your chubby lass can be the belle of class," but I assure you that was not the case. I smiled a lot as a survival tactic, hoping no one would beat me up. It was hard for me to outrun anyone, given my asthma. All this smiling landed me "best personality" in my high school yearbook, which stunned all of my friends and me, most of all. We had assumed no one but my friends knew I existed. I was the reader of the group and read widely, if not with any plan. My favorite books in no special order were the *Catcher in the Rye, Everything You Always Wanted to Know About Sex* (*But Were*

Afraid to Ask), The Diary of Malcolm X, and *The Diary of Anne Frank*. I read *Everything You Always Wanted to Know* any time my parents were out. I knew exactly where it was in their bedroom drawer.

While we had no creative writing classes, per se, I became a writer of short films as my friend had a Super Eight camera. Our experiments ranged from social satire (*Branches,* a clueless white girl's response to *Roots*) and what we thought were experimental mood pieces about our country's consumption that involved close-ups of dripping fat under a hamburger on an outdoor grill. I remember making a gladiator Ken doll as a final project for Ancient History. He came with a foil shield and a neighbor's toy fire truck refashioned as a chariot. My friend and I concocted an elaborate horse costume out of cardboard, pillows, and a broom because we refused to dress as pilgrims or Indians for our school's Thanksgiving festival. Budding pacifists, we had no desire to create the violence upon which our country was founded. We somehow managed to walk to school wearing our equine costume without getting run over by cars and buses. Like many young people, I kept a series of angst-ridden "secret" diaries with little padlocks on them. While so many of my experiences seem now to also lend themselves to poetry, I was not writing any poetry. Because I grew up in New England, in English classes we read Robert Frost and Emily Dickinson. Of course, they were dead, like Robert Louis Stevenson, which bolstered my erroneous notion that no one alive wrote poetry anymore.

I went to the University of Rhode Island, the big state school, voted "best party school" by *Playboy* in 1979, the year I was accepted. I was terrified of frat parties after I saw a flaming couch being thrown out of a frat house window. I had a dorm roommate who blared Cheap Trick cassettes. She was fond of singing "I Want You To Want Me" off key into her hairbrush while doing dance moves. Because of the noise and the smoke from her joints, I spent a lot of time in the bookstore and library. It was there that I found Kathleen Spivack's *The Jane Poems*, a series of very small poems under fifteen lines about an "every woman" named Jane. I had a poetry awakening, bringing me back to *A Child's Garden of Verses*. It was then that I started going through the poetry section of the university library, teaching myself what I could. I fell in love with Dylan Thomas, especially the ending of "Fern Hill"—Time held me green and dying / Though I sang in my chains like the sea.

Just as I was learning that poems didn't have to rhyme, that they were alive with the now, my sister was in a terrible car accident. I made it through just one year at University of Rhode Island and went home, where my sister was now the one in the hospital. It was only then that I started to have an understanding of what my parents had been through with me, driving to Providence every day for visits, rearranging their work schedules and so on. My sister was in a coma from which we were not sure she would return. She missed the end of her senior year of high school, where she was decidedly popular, slim, and an A student to boot. I remember the stitches all over her face, the dry shampoo the nurses used to try to get the blood out of her hair. My parents and I spoke to her because the doctor said that it was possible that on some level she could hear us. I wrote terrible poems that I recited to her, realizing I didn't ever want to go back to University of Rhode Island. When she came out of her coma, my sister asked for ice cream. When the doctor asked questions, she could tell him her name and recite our home phone number. She didn't know what year it was, though she said she'd just turned six. The experience was terrifying in just about every way, but slowly her memory came back and she aged herself back to seventeen.

I moved back in with my parents and sister, resuming my high school job at a shoe store next door to the city's library. I'd go there on my lunch break to the poetry stacks. It was on one such break that I saw a flyer about a study abroad program in Wales. I knew that was where Dylan Thomas was from and made my application. I left in January of 1981 to study in Trinity College in Carmarthen, Wales. It was the first time I'd been on an airplane, the first time I had a passport, the first time I had traveler's checks pinned in my bra. My uncle had given me $800 to cover the costs not met by my shoe store savings and financial aid. Once in Wales, I took a class with Raymond Garlick, a poet in his own right, who taught a class in Welsh Studies. He was an expert on Dylan Thomas and we visited Thomas's grave at St. Martin's. I remember reading more than writing, as I'd lost the confidence and ease with which my ten-year-old self composed narratives. But read I did. I could recite Thomas's "The force that through the green fuse drives the flower "by heart.

After I'd returned home, I transferred to Emerson College in Boston where there was an actual major in Creative Writing. In my first Emerson class, I felt like I was with my people, the misfits, the outliers, the weirdoes who, like me, were trying to figure it all out. I was especially excited to meet Bill Knott, whose work reminded me of Thomas's in its unapologetic passion and strange juxtapositions. The first time I met Bill was at a poetry reading at a Boston bookstore. I got to the bookstore early and recognized Bill from his author's photo though I'd yet to take a class with him. I approached to ask if he was Bill Knott and he said, "I am most definitely NOT Bill Knott" and walked away fidgeting. After the reading, I waited in line to get my book signed and said, "You ARE Bill Knott." He proceeded to cross out whole poems in a purple pen and complained I'd bought his weakest book to date.

At Emerson, Knott's office door was papered with rejection letters. His briefcase was a brown paper bag from a grocery store. He was an outlier in the best sense of the word—not part of any poetry school, not *wanting* to be part of any school. He was generous to a fault and when my first book came out, he bought twenty copies full price and passed them out to his students as gifts. He told his undergraduate student that we should be sending out our poems. And one of his assignments was to produce a rejection letter . . . or an acceptance . . . from a literary magazine by the end of the semester. Over the years we kept in touch and he'd often send chapbooks he'd made himself with a rubber band as a makeshift spine.

My other teachers included Denis Leary (yes, that one—but before he was a famous comedian) and Jack Gantos. Denis Leary gave us all free passes to the comedy clubs where he was perfecting his act. Then we'd meet to talk about his routine—where he got the laughs, where the audience seemed to lose him, how far he could go with any given topic. His material could be raunchy, mean, taboo. It was his students' job to monitor the precise moments people laughed and the precise moments they started to groan or worse began to carry on private conversations. Watching the makings of a comic and comic timing was fascinating to me. There were several poets in that class as well as students studying comedy and acting, and it was amazing to me how fluid the crossover of techniques was from one genre to the other, though it took me a few years to integrate what I'd learned.

Jack Gantos, best known for his children's and young adult titles, taught a class in which we wrote a collaborative novel. It was an eye-opening experience. We all submitted outlines and by sheer luck, he picked mine. The novel was based on my high school friends, but each member of the class wrote a chapter then passed it on to the next person, picking up threads and themes made by the earlier writer. It was incredible that the novel turned out nothing like it would have if I'd written it myself—it was so much better! That is when I first began to understand the letting go of the factual "truth" in writing. The experience also planted a seed for my love of literary collaboration.

At Emerson, I had the pleasure of studying with Tom Lux. He was really good with line-by-line editing, word by word examination. Once I used the word "complain" in a poem, which he pointed out was whiny and dull.

"Gripe," he said. "Gripe! Can't you hear the difference?"

He taught me to edit by piling up the same vowel sounds. He was fascinating, and I loved him. In my senior year, he asked me what I was going to do with my life. I said, "I guess I'll continue my waitressing at the Pru or maybe get a job at the bank." I had no career goals except to be a published poet, which I knew from Bill Knott was not a money-making endeavor. Maybe I could be a substitute teacher. After I listed my listless job ideas, Tom told me I should apply to this thing called an MFA. "An MFwhat?"

I began the MFA at Sarah Lawrence College in the fall of 1985. In addition to studying with Lux, Michael Burkhard, Jean Valentine, and Jane Cooper, I was getting another education at the Nuyorican Poets Café with the likes of Bob Holman, Dangerous Diane, Paul Beaty, Hal Sirowitz, and Jennifer Blowdryer. Sarah Lawrence at that time questioned whether slam poetry was even poetry and the poets at the Nuyorican were, for the most part, horrified by academia and MFA programs. But I slid from one community to the other—there was so much to learn from both. I was learning craft at Sarah Lawrence, trying to tighten my rambling lines. I was learning how to put politics in my poems at the Nuyorican. Valentine and Cooper were my first female poetry mentors and the voices of the Nuyorican gave me the guts to put the issues I was always talking about with my friends in my poems.

It had been a lifelong dream of mine to live in New York City, and I finally did after one semester as a nanny in Bronxville. My first apartment was on 1st Avenue and 1st Street with a depressed but likeable roommate. The tenement was dark with no natural light. My bedroom window had a view of a brick wall from the building next door less than a foot away. A shower stall in the kitchen. Cockroaches in the sink. But I wasn't discouraged—I was living in a space with the same floor plan as those described in William S. Burrough's *Junkie*. Frank O'Hara quickly became my muse. I wrote a poem a day based on my walks to and from the subway. I volunteered in a soup kitchen for The Catholic Worker. I fell in and out of love with questionable characters—an alcoholic painter, a slam poet from

Brooklyn, a coldhearted computer techie—each one breaking my heart but giving me material for my poems.

I went to the Guggenheim on the days it was free. Every Saturday I went to an early art house movie at Angelika's or The Quad, paid for one ticket, then went from theater to theater and stayed until it was dark outside. New York City itself was like a movie. I made friends with a woman who was an extra in almost all of Woody Allen's films. I made friends with a cast member of *Saturday Night Live*. My childhood friend from Woonsocket had also moved to New York where he worked for a talent agent. He took me to all kinds of premiers as his plus one. He even took me to a party at Eric Roberts' apartment where my friend was trying to sign Julia Roberts also. Here is a prophesy of mine that flopped. "Julia will never be a star," I said. "She seems really dull." I met James Elroy before he became famous, around the time of his book third book *Blood on the Moon*. I palled around with playwright Suzanne Lori Parks before she won the Pulitzer.

After I moved to a slightly less awful tenement on Avenue B, *Beaches* was filmed on my street. Barbara Hershey drove a green van, Bette Midler in a bunny suit in the passenger seat. A white van crawled ahead of them with a boom mike sticking out the back. I danced at Area. I danced at the Limelight. I saw Annie Sprinkle at The Pyramid. I saw Sandra Bernhard on the street then at her one-woman show *Without You, I'm Nothing* at the Orpheum Theater on Second Avenue. I ate a lot of cheap Indian food on First Street. I ate hundreds of soy burgers at Dojo's, one of the most inexpensive meals in the whole city. The reason I mention all this is because New York was an education of a different kind and all of it infused my poetry.

I worked low-level advertising jobs, as a receptionist in a fancy rug store in Soho, as a receptionist again in a health club for women. I worked as a tutor on the set of *Kate & Allie*. Jane Curtin always sent me for coffee never realizing I wasn't her assistant. But I was so starstruck I'd walk out of the Ed Sullivan Theater (where the TV show was taped) and get her whatever she wanted. My student was Allison Smith, who played one of Curtin's (Allie's) kids. She had to have her hair cut less than a centimeter every week so that the show would have continuity. I helped her study for the SATs—I was impressed that she knew the definition of "flatiron" though I didn't. Susan St. James (Kate) was pregnant my last year there and they hid her stomach in a bubble bath. There was one take of her where you could see she was actually pregnant that the directors used in a flashback. I taught composition as an adjunct at NYU, Baruch, LaGuardia College, and Rutgers. When I read at the final Sarah Lawrence student reading, I met my poet friend Maureen Seaton who was there to listen to someone else. We became fast friends and in a few years began our collaborative poems. She was the first poet with whom I took the plunge. Since then, I have collaborated with others, including Sandy McIntosh, Amy Lemmon, and Julie Marie Wade.

I stayed in New York after my graduation, pretty much doing the same jobs I did when I was in grad school. My poetry friend Page Delano and I won our first poetry grants—a New York Foundation for the Arts Fellowship—in 1989. I remember Page bought a really nice coat and I bought a pink neon POET sign. This was in the days of affirmations and New Age rhetoric. Some part of me was making fun of that idea and another part was earnest—if I had a pink flashing POET sign, I must be a poet, right? One day when my window was open, I heard a man's voice calling, "Hey poet!" I stuck my head out of the grimy window and below me on the sidewalk stood Jim Feast, a member of the Unbearables. He headed a posse of great poets who did a mimeographed magazine *The National Poetry Magazine of the Lower East Side* and invited me to bring copies of one of my poems to ABC No Rio where a group of us would collate them. It reminded me of the joy I had making books at the children's hospital. But in this venture, a visual artist would design a front and back cover and then staple everything together. Each poet got a copy and then we sold the rest on consignment at St. Mark's Bookstore.

I walked the Brooklyn Bridge under a full moon. I had my picture taken with Bill Murray at a party. I "slammed" at the Nuyorican Poet's Café. I "slammed" at CBGB's. Soon I moved from Avenue B to 23rd Street, right across the street from the historic Chelsea Hotel, where my beloved Dylan Thomas spent some of his last days on earth. "Queen of Mean" Leona Helmsley was my slumlord and, because of some lucky loophole, I didn't have to pay rent for a few months in 1989 when she was being convicted of tax evasion.

I celebrated my 30th birthday in Central Park. It was June of 1991. My friends and I tied some balloons to a tree. We sat on blankets with a pink frosted cake. I blew out the candles, probably wishing for fame as a poet. Bobby Rivers had just read one of my poems on VH1—I secretly hoped that alone would lead to immortality. But, of course, I still had a long way to go.

Geoffrey O'Brien

Lynne
Thompson

Alfred Corn

Arthur Sze

Sheila E. Murphy

Burt
Kimmelman

Geoffrey O'Brien

Where Did Poetry Come From

Two Early Encounters

1.

> Diddle diddle dumpling
> My son John
> Went to bed
> With his stockings on
> One shoe off
> And the other shoe on
> Diddle diddle dumpling
> My son John

A woman's voice is speaking it.

She knows what comes next. Her voice expresses the pleasure of knowing it. Anticipates your pleasure. Anticipates her own pleasure at being about to shape the sounds yet one more time.

The sounds were once uttered to her in the same fashion. By which utterance she was in part fashioned. As she now in turn is fashioning. A cycle becomes apparent to her in the rounded motion of it rolling in its grooves. Molding with molded sounds. Giving form to air. Counting out, as an accompaniment to touching, an extension of touching.

Contact.

The occasion of the rhyme is an infant's bedtime. It marks a transition. It masks a transition. It masks an interruption. It distracts from the intrusion of being lifted out of play, hauled into the disagreeable discipline of having free movement restricted, of going through all the stages of washing and undressing and being put into bed and given over to darkness.

A break point approaches. Soon the mouth of a cavern will swallow the room and all it holds.

A woman's voice. It could have been a man's voice but in memory never was. Not speaking but half chanting and half teasing. It is the sound of an intimate knowledge of the inside of the body. A sound of love or what sounds like love, of a desire to give comfort. Of the pleasure of sharing what is almost too silly to be said aloud. Of a holy and inane abandonment.

Diddle

What is diddle. What does diddle look like? Like nothing at all. It is the sound of some unsuspected capacity hidden in the mouth.

Diddle diddle

The action of the tongue moving back and forth against the top of the mouth. Just shy of where the teeth start. A ticklish repetition that could go on forever.

Dumpling

A round and busy sound, closing together and popping apart. Funny in itself and pleasurable to say again and again. A sound shaped like the mouth. And a thing, something remembered and desired, a foodstuff *scrumptious*, word in which the texture of a dumpling in the mouth joins with the imagined flavor now permeating the sound of the word and the part the word plays in the rhythm of what is being put forth, in a place liberated from constraint and permanently surprising and pleasing. And somewhere inside it, on the reverse side of its syllables if you could follow them that far back, perhaps the surprise of having a body at all.

My son John

Three even claps. Whose son? Who's John? Who speaks? Another infant entering another bed. Everything has already happened before. In the place across the way, wherever that way might be, the way where the words have already been, the country where they went pioneering, in the rhyme where everything that long ago happened is happening again. It happened and so the words are shaped this way. Everything that happens now *must* happen because it already did. Is in movement and can no longer be stopped.

Went to bed
With his stockings on

Heard before understood. Memorized before understood. A picture formed without asking why or how. The ruts of its sounds familiar like floorboards many times crawled over. A story told before any sense of what a story was. Why did it happen. Was it shameful that it happened? So shameful or ridiculous or miraculous that a rhyme was made of it.

One shoe off

The clomp of a shoe falling to the floor. Hitting the floor on the last beat.

And the other shoe on

An answer coming back, from other to one. A dance taking place, tilting back and forth from off to on. As if seesawing in a basket. A basket of contradictions. One on, other off. Light off, night on.

Diddle diddle dumpling
My son John

Falling now not rising. The same words coming back only to say that this time it's over—once was to open, twice to close—the utterance snaps shut, ending where it started, returned inside itself. Swaddled in night. Engulfed.

Finally, it will rise again to the surface as an inner voice, if not the voice of the listener then a voice that installed itself within, reciting what never needed to be memorized. It nudged its way into memory, finding by stealth a place already established for it. Where it will now continue to repeat itself. Perhaps for the pleasure of it. Pleasure on the part of who or what. Living machinery that plays its own music to itself. In any event not to be evicted.

To be joined by so many more, they will rattle around together, rhymes with crumbs of stories in them, the tales of Mother Hubbard's poor dog and Peter the pumpkin eater and the woman in the gigantic shoe, the cadaverous husband and the enormous plump wife, of the mouse and the clock and the dish and the moon, of Jack and Jill and their disastrous fate at the bottom of hill. Not tales at all since you can never know anything further of them or what happened before or after, nothing actually of what any of this is about beyond its own grotesque fragmentary reality. Something simply was and was imprinted. The rhyme is proof of its finality.

Comforting because known, if for no other reason. Even if not chosen, somehow at home in the world of pails and shoes and barking dogs and water buckets. Of knocks and cracks and frights worn away into harmlessness, now merely odd, messages from beings who can say this and nothing more, which is like saying nothing. Why did they fall? Who had ever known them?

Not tales but shreds of sound. Pieces of thump.

See saw Marjory Daw

Pease porridge in the pot

Some in rags and some in tags

Alive only in the satisfaction of the edge of the tongue hitting the spot, to make the sound come right, any obstacle having been taken out of the way. Passage made clear.

And the beat ever after to be heard underneath at the bottom of it

Ding dong bell

Full fathom five

Fee fi fo fum

Tweedledee and Tweedledum

Boomlay boomlay boomlay boom

2.

> dark brown is the river
>   golden is the sand
> it flows along forever
>   with trees on either hand
>
> green leaves a-floating
>   castles of the foam
> boats of mine a-boating
>   where will all come home
>
> on goes the river
>   and out past the mill
> away down the valley
>   away down the hill
>
> away down the river
>   a hundred miles or more
> other little children
>   shall bring my boats ashore

There were phrases found in Robert Louis Stevenson that stuck like pictures in a book seen once and never after unseen, returned to out of need

> my bed is a boat
> I never can get back by day
> the trees are crying aloud
> all night across the dark we steer
> to Providence or Babylon
> shivering in my nakedness
> see the spreading circles die
> cities blazing in the fire

The terrors of night for once spoken aloud, the power of fires and shadows.

And by morning light other words

hayloft

meadow-side

wagons

mill wheel

Made of straw and weathered wood, pictures of a scarcely known world. World continuous with sun and ground and hedge.

In this book, handed down in an already crinkled copy, crayon marks in its margins, what was hidden was being revealed. A constant opening up. Nobody knew of these things except Robert Louis Stevenson. First named author. Secret voice, intimate presence.

The words are places and in the middle of them—the middle of themselves—they want to move beyond into other places

I should like to rise and go
where the golden apples grow

And that is enough. The words can stop right there, stay forever on that rising note, suspended until they find themselves where everything has been all along, staring into water, the cool water always to be found lapping at the edge of the hiding place under some bridge, the edge of some clear stream

O the clean gravel!

A child makes boats out of paper. The boats are set floating in a stream and go out of sight and are lost. They are not lost. They will find a harbor among other children. Unknown children in an unknown world.

The children are not there. They are not to be seen. They are other. Who are they anyway? They are somewhere. On the other side. After the words end.

Where does poetry come from

Where Go the Boats?

Lynne Thompson

Father Tongue

I.

My journey to becoming a writer was inspired by my father who was a storyteller and a closet poet (because Mother saw no point in any effort that netted no money). He gave me a lifelong love of a narrative wrapped in evocative language; insisted on a life spent "looking" and capturing those observations in crisp and elegant English, despite his immigrant status.

> . . . . . . Daddy could bring the heat—although
> he never would have said *bring the heat*
> because his home rule kind of schooling
> favored the King's English over the colloquial.

Anyway, when he told me he had only months of life left after years of unfiltered Camel cigarettes, as he dragged a contraption filled with oxygen behind him, the ribbony plastic of it piercing his nose, his breathing labored, his future behind him, Daddy asked me to drive him back through the old neighborhoods. More specifically, my father asked me to take him to see the four houses we had lived in together and I knew—although only vaguely—he was asking me to remember—to tell—his stories after he was gone.

His invitation was a big deal. He didn't ask any of the four sons who will always be the children who came along before me. He didn't ask his wife. Perhaps he knew she would make reminiscing difficult. He asked me who will always be the daughter not of his body but of his heart.

> [my] new parents, having consented in court
> and signed all the papers (blah and more legal

blah) hereby & henceforth would, in all cases,
respect and treat the minor as their child . . ."

Perhaps he knew I would write of our journey one day. As he could no longer drive without the danger of killing himself and others, perhaps it was just a matter of convenience and proximity. Truth is, I no longer recall—if I ever knew—his reason, and because I am a writer, perhaps I've made this all up.Truth is, neither he nor I could recall the home he first lived in when he arrived in Los Angeles in the 1930s. He'd come to Chicago via New York via Barbados, traveling alone, not knowing what lay ahead for him. I imagine he might have thought:

> "I left that floating hotel, the *Van Dyck*, to arrive—via
> Barbados—on the Isle of Tears, June 1923, and I didn't
> care what. We'd heard the news back home about a black
> man, Sam Hose, lynched for killing his Georgia white
> employer. Hose was burned alive, knuckles put up or sale
> and *that'll teach 'em* at the local grocer's, but I came anyway . . ."

Perplexed by the conundrum that he found to be America, and after he contracted pneumonia, he drove from Chicago to Los Angeles *before* the publication of *The Negro Traveler's Green Book*—the guide only briefly mentioned in the eponymous award-winning movie—that was meant to ensure a degree of safety for mid-20th-century Negro travelers. When I wanted to reimagine what his journey must have entailed, I could only think of how dangerous it must have been, of how courageous my father was.

> For a bite to eat in Amarillo, he would
> have been given a tip: "try Tom's Place,
> New Harlem, or Blue Bonnet" and so on
> across the country. He had no guide; had
> only the risk of rope in Oklahoma City
> or Santa Fe, N.M. . . .

Daddy couldn't remember his first LA residence—although family legend had it that he worked as a chauffeur for a German movie director and perhaps he lived in the director's home—I was wishing it was

Ernst Lubitsch; you know, "Ninotchka" but I could never prove it—so we started our journey, 1974, with the first house I ever shared with him. It sits—still—on Virgil Avenue where it shares a corner with Middlebury. The way I remember it—

> [t]he house that was my first was a house
> that Daddy brought to Virgil atop a flat-
>
> bed truck. He made his boys fix it to the
> foundation, then do whatever else was
> needed to create a kind of permanence.

He didn't say much as we drove by but he also looked like a man returning to a place he could never return to. In my eyes, the old home was *so* much smaller than I recalled it. I'm told that's because children's eyes are a variation on rear view mirrors: objects in the mirror may be smaller than you remember. So, to me, the house not only looked small; it looked like a disaster. The side yard I remembered my brothers so diligently tending was crammed with what our mother would have called junk. And the house itself sat so perilously close to the street as to deny any two people who may have wanted to from walking side by side.

Still, this recreated permanence didn't prevent Daddy from maintaining a connection to his homeland in the West Indies. Every Sunday, we drove

> down Vine Street, past Forest
> Lawn Cemetery, to Griffith
> Park, where Daddy, nutmeg-
> colored and clad head-to-toe
> in his all-whites, came to play

II

It didn't take us long to drive from Virgil Avenue to Victoria Avenue to view our second home, the one we moved to before I was old enough to attend school. My father finally got what he'd long wanted: a house set back from the street, a house wearing a beautiful green "lawn skirt", and he drew extra gulps of air from his oxygen tank when he saw it again. In the backyard, which we could spy when we turned my car around in the driveway, was the ever-bountiful avocado tree and the backyard where my father and brothers constructed a swing-set for me. It was all very post-World War II America—or at least that's the story the family promoted. We were living a million miles away from the homes my father and mother had left in St. Vincent and the Grenadines. It was a million miles away Money, Mississippi and Emmett Till, from Montgomery, Alabama and Rosa Parks. It was a home my parents could afford—thanks to any-Negro-during-the-war-is-eligible Harry Truman who "allowed" black folks to work in the defense industry which led to my father working as an engineer at Lockheed Aircraft and my brother attending a school he could never have attended but for *Brown vs. Board of Education.*

I didn't know if our family was rich or poor but it didn't matter because in Los Angeles, the familiar is always being knocked down and one day, an unfamiliar man came to see my father. They were having one of those "stay in your room" types of conversations. I did not stay in my room. Instead, I spied on the man and my father from the staircase and although I didn't completely understand what they were saying, it was going to come clear soon enough:

> "Yessir", City Hall said, "L.A.s going
> to build the I-10 freeway right through
> the molding of your living room, but
> we'll make you and yours a fine offer
> to move along . . . I mean, to relocate."

So the house he loved, like so many other houses that were thought to be expendable, was going to be subject to a wrecking ball though I was, then, too innocent to know how to describe our disappointment in words. What I knew was that Victoria Avenue was going to be sacrificed so that President Eisenhower could build the interstate highway he envisioned although he didn't envision it going through the moneyed neighborhoods of Hancock Park, Beverly or Cheviot Hills. Ike (or his minions) envisioned the interstate dividing neighborhoods: north and south, haves / have-nots, color and no-color. Ike succeeded but when daddy and I finally made our drive, the house on Victoria was still standing—"highway be damned". Nevertheless,

The brothers say [we] were better off than
many. [We] were the ones with a drum.

I turned the wheel south to the home my father purchased, after.

III

The City's eminent domain money was, I assume, substantial—substantial enough for my father to purchase a home in a once-all-white neighborhood known as View Park. An unincorporated suburb of Los Angeles, View Park's architecture rivaled the architecture of other "whites-only" homes one could find in Los Angeles and that satisfaction glistened on my mother's cheeks—she of the mixed race, the "other white meat". Years later, I learned that when my parents first inquired about the home on Aureola Boulevard, they were told by the broker that a sale to them was prohibited by a restrictive covenant although one of the brothers told me that much more veiled language was used. It was the homeowner—enlightened or anxious—who called the broker to say that he would welcome my parents as potential purchasers of the home. And purchase they did. When we moved in, I got a new Schwinn bicycle so what did I care there were no other Negro families living on the street? I was eager—weren't the neighbors equally as eager—to meet the girls I saw looking out of their windows in the house that faced ours.

The woman in the window is a dead ringer for
Donna Reed. Minutes ago, she sent her reasons

for living safely off: her husband with his flask
of milk, his Dragnet special; their daughters with

Heidi-hefty curls of gold; their sons perched atop
their Schwinns and armed with news about some

preacher named King; her man's *don't take chances*
drumming in her ears—*avoid the windows and lock
the doors.*

Father couldn't have been surprised but he feigned no memory of any of it as we drove by the old Aureola home, then painted a garish orange and much less attractive than when we had lived behind its green-and-white façade.

When I reminded him of one of the brother's stories about his boss from Lockheed Aircraft Company showing up, unannounced, on the pretext of asking my father to fix an old radio while actually evaluating his living conditions, Daddy just smiled and said how happy mother had been to move to a wide tree-lined "boo-lee-vard" (per mother's Carib-inflicted pronunciation); said it was his favorite home among all the homes that he had ever lived in. He reminded me of the ups-and-downs of it: that we'd stocked canned goods because of the Bay of Pigs debacle in Cuba, that we'd learned about a country called Vietnam half-way around the world without really learning what was happening there, that two of his sons—my brothers—married in that house and not long before the Reverend Dr. King had a dream; that President Kennedy had been killed and a dream called Camelot died when we lived in that house.

While my father engaged in this reverie, I recalled that it was this house where I began to question who I would be as a woman, began to question what my parents wanted me to be.

> You might expect as centerpiece
> *West Indian Village With Figures*
>
> *Dancing.* Instead, my immigrant
> parents buy a European imitation,
>
> hang *Bal du Moulin de la Galette*
> in our vestibule. All I can ask is
>
> *are these the women you both pray*
> *I will be?*

IV

When his last two sons began their married lives, the house on Aureola was too big for him, my mother, and me, so our now-reduced family moved again, minutes away to house number four: a quaint English-style bungalow on Escalon Avenue in Windsor Hills. It was in this house that my father came to terms with the contraction and expansion of his family, with the departure of his children, the arrival of his grandchildren. Happily, he said he was grateful for the garage where he could store his nuts and bolts and screwdrivers so he was ready to fix whatever needed fixing (although after he died, I could only find innocuous vestiges of his pleasures among his belongings.)

> Daddy left us a box
> made for tie tacks
> that contained
> no tie tacks
> contained one yellow
> screwdriver
> a government badge . . .
> a light bulb
> too small
> to light anything

He reminded me how fond he was of the avocado tree that was also a favorite of our dog, Sky, our constant family companion since I'd been a girl. That avocado tree yielded fruit that turned Sky's coat to silk.

> Forepaw arched, eyes eager, I set upon the day's
> sparrow as a swallow tail lands upon a limb
> of box elder, hovers, unnoticed, until—
>
> It is late summer when avocados ripen to bursting
> and run and laugh are everything.
> "In My Summer as a Weimaraner".

Daddy remembers that he retired when we came to live in the Escalon house. He remembers that Tante Ida—the matriarch of our family in America—also retired. came to live with us in that house and that Tante had had a stroke in the den while watching a sitcom: Bewitched (which she must have been because she made America possible for all of us.)

> He say: remember ya auntie
> The last queen before the queen
> that was your mother? The last proper,
> her legs crossed just above her ankles?
> She bought you throne. Bought it
> with her strong black thighs.

Not long after the move to Escalon, I left Los Angeles to attend College. My father and mother were—at long last—alone. I don't know what they said to each other, what it was no longer important to say. I imagine it must have been strange because before I could collect a degree, my mother telephoned to say that the Escalon home was sold and she and my father were moving to an apartment in Culver City, a suburb of Los Angeles. There would be a room for me, she said, if I needed one—and I did.

> Their unmarried daughter, who's asked to
> come home, again, understands less than less.
>
> Comes the dawn and the wife attends
> to rote duties: her husband's breathing
>
> apparatus in need of its regular click;
> the dog scratching to be let outdoors.

V

I moved into the apartment in Culver City after College graduation; the last home my father would share with us. When my father wasn't in the hospital, he sat on the apartment's balcony, eating bowls of ice cream that he waited to melt into a kind of milkshake. He liked to play Scrabble because language, he said, was the thing that made a difference to one's ability to get ahead in this world. For the first time, I saw my mother smoke a cigarette.

My father never complained about any of it. Eventually, I moved to my own apartment a few blocks away and my father implored me to never let my membership in the Automobile Club of Southern California lapse. He insisted that he would never die surrounded by nurses (even though they brought him the Nestle chocolate bars his doctors denied him). He was right. In the apartment with his wife, in a place he never thought of as home, he died but he's still at home with me now. I began to write this memoir on Easter Sunday, 2018, and I remember him, improbably, focusing a small camera, saying *remember this, remember it all,* taking his shot:

> with me, on the end—all candy-stripped ribbons,
> scarred knees, little hope; our virtues trapped by a
> Brownie. Does anyone know what that means
> anymore? Do we rise?

———

All excerpted lines are contained in poems published in Fretwork, *my collection selected by Jane Hirshfield as the winner of the 2019 Marsh Hawk Press Poetry Prize.*

Alfred Corn

A Writer's Beginnings

BIOGRAPHICAL CRITICS HAVE PROPOSED that artists always have in their background a psychological wound that explains why they choose (if it is a matter of choice) a vocation sourced in emotional displacements. If this is true, I can cite a fact that might qualify: the death of my mother on my second birthday, an event that could only have been traumatic even though I have no conscious memories of it. Art is made not solely with emotion, however. Knowledge and skill also come into the process, and, after that, the chances that bring us to the right place at the right time, where we meet the right people. It's not possible to know how many artists having a suitably emotional psychology and an education sufficient to give them the knowledge and technical skill needed for artistic production even so did not emerge because they were in the wrong place or the wrong time, and therefore did not meet people who could help them find their way. I was lucky.

After a few years in elementary school, it became clear that I was good at my subjects. From that time on, I made the highest grades given in my classes. I had learned to read a little from my older sisters and tended to follow with whatever texts they might have in hand. I had a taste of Beatrix Potter, *The Secret Garden*, Laura Ingalls Wilder's "Little House on the Prairie" series, and Lewis Carroll's two Alice books. A bit later I discovered the Grimm fairy tales and Greek mythology. Still later I began reading Poe's tales and reread them many times, even though some of them filled me with dread. *The Swiss Family Robinson, Treasure Island, Robinson Crusoe*, and *Gulliver's Travels* were other books I read. This will sound quaint nowadays, but we had a family custom of reading "A Visit from St. Nicholas" on Christmas Eve, just before we went to sleep; later on, I added to that an annual rereading of Dickens' *A Christmas Carol*. Of course, there was a Bible reading at church, and part of every Sunday

School lesson was memorizing a few verses of the King James translation. Some of these I still have by heart.

In high school, I always looked forward and remembered reading Shakespeare's *Julius Caesar* during my freshman year with something like awe. We were required to memorize several passages from it and I still know them, along with several of his sonnets. In the next years I read *Romeo and Juliet* and *Macbeth*, and these fascinated me as well.

Our English textbook also contained selections from English and American poetry, and I recall feeling special admiration for Keats, Emily Dickinson, and Whitman. At one point I even bought a little paperback of Whitman's poetry, one of the "Laurel" series, under Richard Wilbur's directorship. Poems rendering passional and sexual feeling made a deep impression on me, and, when I read the section from the second edition of *Leaves of Grass* that begins, "Hours continuing long, sore, and heavy-hearted," a wild surmise shot through me: Was it possible that this poet, too . . . . ? One day our English teacher asked the students which genre they preferred, prose or poetry? I was the only class member raising his hand to vote for the chosen genre of Shakespeare and Whitman.

I soon found my way to Louis Untermeyer's anthology of contemporary American verse (no longer especially contemporary by the time I got to it) and read through the selections with fascination. I liked almost everything indiscriminately—Vachel Lindsay, Amy Lowell, Edna Saint-Vincent Millay, Sara Teasdale, Elinor Wylie, Conrad Aiken, H.D., at least some of Eliot, very little of Pound, but all the many selections from Wallace Stevens. Untermeyer's was the early, quasi-Imagiste Stevens, and I've learned the value of his later poems even more. Yet his stately cadences were, as soon as I read them, engraved in my memory: "Beauty is momentary in the mind— / The fitful tracing of a portal; / But in the flesh it is immortal." True, there were also poems in a lighter, more fanciful vein, "Chieftain Iffucan of Azcan in caftan / Of tan and henna hackles, halt!" or "The only emperor is the emperor of ice-cream." The strange thing is that Stevens's reputation in that day was relatively small. I don't remember any poem of his being taught, a few years later, in my college English courses. The emphasis was all on Eliot, whom I sometimes liked ("The Love Song of J. Alfred Prufrock") and sometimes didn't ("The Waste Land"). My love for Stevens stayed in hiding, like some embarrassing, childish enthusiasm.

I also read prose fiction: *Silas Marner, David Copperfield, Vanity Fair,*

Of Human Bondage, East of Eden. There was no method to my reading. I would go to the small local Carnegie Library and simply take out whatever was on the shelf. Exactly what percentage of these works' content I grasped, who can say? Considering that I worked my way through the entire Bible, perhaps it's also credible that, at age fifteen or sixteen, I read every page of *War and Peace*, which took a year, off and on. Again, I couldn't follow half its intentions, but characters like Natasha and Anatole made a lasting impression, and especially Pierre, with whom I identified as another well-meaning and intelligent but bumbling outsider.

I began foreign language study with Latin in my freshman and sophomore years, then French in my junior and senior years. There was something magical about reading another language; no one had to persuade me to make the effort. I would have liked to take more Latin, but our school only offered two years of it. On the other hand, I especially liked French because, in addition to reading, you could also speak it, which was a new form of entertainment. A piece of luck for me was that the local college, Valdosta State, engaged a native Frenchman, a Breton named Jean Guitton, who came to address our class. He it was who taught me to get right the pronunciation of the French *u* and *r*, those stumbling blocks for most beginning students. My classmates regarded me with a mixture of disdain and envy since no one else could even come close; but then, to us Americans, foreign languages are so *weird*.

Lest this all sound too grand—the formative years of Little Lord Intelloroy—I should also report that I read my parent's Book-of-the-Month Club (or was it Reader's Digest Lest this all sound too grand—the formative years of Little Lord Intelloroy—I should also report that I read my parent's Book-of-the-Month Club (or was it Reader's Digest Condensed Books?) selections, forgotten Fifties best-sellers like *The Robe* and *Marjorie Morningstar* and *Peyton Place*. As a good white southerner, I read *Gone with the Wind*, and (even at age eleven) understood all of it, though I hadn't been been sensitized to its fundamental racist assumptions. I thought Margaret Mitchell must have loved the character Mammy. Perhaps she did, but it was love unaccompanied by much understanding.

Another weekly item of reading was *Life* magazine, whose articles I scrutinized (or, at least, its famous photographs), sometimes shaking my head in disbelief at, for example, a piece on the Beat Generation. Which surely had to be exaggerated, no one could *ever* want to live like that, not really! I also remember a cover showing an explosion of the hydrogen bomb. That may be the point at which it was impressed on me that America had a mortal enemy in the Soviet Union; and that nuclear war could destroy us all. In a fundamentalist culture, this eventuality was conflated with the eschatology outlined in the prophecies of *Revelation*. The Bible said God would send a rain of fire to put an end to our sinful world, and here at last the means of doing so had become available. (Did that imply, then, that atheist Communism was ordained as God's specially appointed servant and executioner? The question was never raised.) Around the same time, I read John Hersey's *Hiroshima*, which made the actuality of nuclear destruction horribly and concretely available to imagination, the source of several nightmares and an underlying dread that ran through all my young adult years. Not only was I forced to know at an early age that I was going to die, I now knew that human civilization itself was mortally endangered.

Hollywood's dream machines come even to the smallest towns, dispensing tragedy, triumph, and laughter. Hardly a week went by that we didn't see whatever movie (we called them "pictures") the Ritz theater was showing. When I was little, I went on Saturday afternoons by myself and got to hear Johnny Weissmuller's Tarzan yodel and see his animal-skin loincloth. I saw westerns with Gene Autry, Gabby Hayes, and Roy Rogers, the Ma and Pa Kettle movies, Abbot and Costello, and the Three Stooges. When I was older, the family usually went together, say, on a Friday evening. Then we took in *On the Waterfront, Marty, All About Eve, Sabrina, Written on the Wind, Picnic, Psycho, North by Northwest, The Seven Year Itch, East of Eden, Pillow Talk, Cinderella, How to Marry a Millionaire, High Noon, Bus Stop*—classics and endless numbers of musicals, including *Showboat* and *Singing in the Rain*. The only movies I didn't like were war pictures, excepting *From Here to Eternity* and *Stalag 17*, which lacked the bloody trench-warfare scenes I found so dull and undramatic.

In my high school you could be exempted from Physical Education courses if you signed up for the student chorus. Dreading four years of excruciating ineptitude at base-, basket- or football, I took up music, one of the luckiest decisions of my life. Apparently I had inherited some of my mother's musical talent; I could sing and soon learned to read music by sight, supplying sound for the notes with my somewhat underpowered baritone. I loved the sensuous, all-embracing quality of music, its quickening rhythm, its access to otherwise unreachable heights of ecstasy or depths of sorrow. I acquired a little portable record player and began checking out classical LPs along with books at the Carnegie Library. At one point, I asked my parents to sponsor piano lessons; they refused. It was expensive, you know, we had no piano, I would soon get bored with it, just as my sisters had. My father probably also thought that this was just one more "unmanly" pursuit that should be discouraged. I was bitterly disappointed, aware even then how paradoxical my situation was—instead of parents pleading with a child to learn to play the piano, here was a child begging his parents for lessons, and being refused.

So, I made up my mind to see what you could learn on your own. Whenever a piano was around, I made tentative explorations among its keys; got books from the library about music and music theory; learned about meter, rhythm, key signatures and harmony. And I began to write little pieces, singing as much as I could of them, playing some of the notes on piano, when I could get near one. It was frustrating, since I couldn't really perform any of my compositions, couldn't give them the ear test. At one point my stepmother came into my room and, seeing a piece of staff paper with notes marked on it, asked me what I was doing. "Writing music," I answered. "But how can you write music, when you can't even play the piano?" "I hear it in my head." (Which was partly true.) At this, she gave me a puzzled, disbelieving look and left the room.

My curious occupation was reported to the rest of the family, who wondered what on earth it could possibly mean. I had my revenge: At some point I showed a keyboard piece to our church organist, who was also our choir director. She and I were friends because I also sang in the church choir. Just out of music school, she was pleased to find someone who adored the art as much as she did. So, she made a few suggestions for revisions, came up with a series of organ stops to use for the piece, and played it as a prelude at church one Sunday morning. My parents were astonished; but it was an important step in their growing realization that I was not an average child, that I had unusual propensities. During my last year of high school, my father sponsored singing lessons for me, which made up for past denials to a degree. But I didn't have a professional-quality voice, just a good addition to a chorus. Meanwhile, there was still no way for me to play the compositions I wrote.

In 1961 I began my first year at Emory University. I elected French literature as my major, a degree requiring study of German and Italian language as well. A major discovery resulting from those studies was the poetry of Dante and Rilke, both important influences on what I would later write. Among other courses I enjoyed was an introduction to philosophy taught by John Wilcox, who took a friendly interest in me after he read a few of my assigned papers. At some point he invited me to dinner—an occasion to meet his wife Patricia, whom I soon learned to call "Pat." She was a poet, if not much published then, and had known other published poets like James Dickey, Edgar Bowers, and Turner Cassity. We began to see each other constantly; she became a sort of mentor, an unpaid tour-guide to contemporary poetry. She had a special admiration for Roethke, and I came to share it. We exchanged poems, my few, haphazard efforts against her own more accomplished ones. For reasons unclear to me, my interest shifted to prose fiction more than to poetry. Possibly that was the result of reading masterpieces of prose fiction I hadn't gotten to before, including *Don Quixote*, Austen, Melville, Kafka, Conrad, and Thomas Mann. It may also be that the fashion of the day was for Eliot and Pound, whose approach to poetry was uncongenial to me. I took a short fiction workshop with H.E. Francis—the only creative writing course I ever enrolled in. It would be nearly a decade before I returned to poetry.

For graduate studies in French literature, I was accepted at Harvard, Yale, Princeton and Columbia. I settled on the last because it was located in New York, where I'd wanted to live for a long time. Why? Because it was the capital of the arts in America. During the years of graduate study my interest in an academic career began to fade, in proportion to an increasing devotion to the arts. My Fulbright fellowship for a year of research in Paris only served to firm up literary ambitions. The work I did there (on the influence relationship between Melville and Camus) never resulted in the dissertation I was meant to write, which would have completed the PhD. degree requirements. I abandoned my studies without it, and also with no concrete plan other than to try to be a writer.

In my second year of graduate school, I happened to meet Edmund White, who, though he hadn't yet published a book, was extraordinarily well read and actively engaged in writing. I found him fascinating, a brilliant and witty conversationalist. We formed an instant friendship, based partly on our shared sexual orientation. His recently completed autobiographical novel was being sent to publishers, but in the 1960s American LGBT literature was in its infancy and had to face considerable resistance. Edmund's efforts amount to literary pioneering. He was the first person of intellect I'd ever met whom I couldn't best in an argument, partly because in almost any discussion he always preferred to take the adversary position. He seemed to know arguments on every side of a question and had excellent debating skills. He became a sort of mentor, pointing me toward this or that writer, taking (to me) strange positions such as the idea that Joyce was overrated and the F. Scott Fitzgerald was a great novelist. As a convinced francophile, I urged him to read Alain Robbe-Grillet and the French *nouveau roman*, so that he would get beyond a "nineteenth century approach to fiction." I was sold on the idea of a purely innovative or avant-garde approach to art—after all, hadn't the greatest artists always been pioneers in their genres? He listened politely and offered counterarguments. Later on, I would see that my rather doctrinaire opinions had nevertheless had an effect.

In October of 1969, Ed White had introduced me to the poet Richard Howard, who seemed willing to take on an apprentice—a service he has performed for scores of aspiring poets and novelists over the past decades. My efforts at writing fiction hadn't come to much, so I took up poetry again. Richard was forbearing and receptive, offering suggestions for reading, including the work of James Merrill, which was unknown to me. *Alone with America*, Richard's critical study of contemporary American poetry, appeared shortly after we met, a fascinating introduction to authors I hadn't yet read, like John Ashbery and John Hollander.

One evening in the spring of 1970 (not long after the announcement that his volume of dramatic monologues *Untitled Subjects* had been awarded the Pulitzer Prize), Richard took me to meet a professor-critic friend of his, who turned out to be David Kalstone. But we didn't see each other again until much later, after Ed White had become a close friend of his. David was an English professor at Rutgers and a regular poetry reviewer for *The New York Times*. He knew a number of poets, including James Merrill, John Ashbery, and Adrienne Rich, all of whom I came to admire. We developed a warm attachment, with David acting as a sort of channel of sensibility and knowledge—not to mention worldly experience. I showed him new poems; he offered gentle reactions to them. We read Elizabeth Bishop and Wallace Stevens aloud and discussed their merits. We attended performances of George Balanchine's New York City Ballet, about which David had expert opinions. Possibly we were reenacting the ancient Greek ideal of *paideia*, in at least in some of its aspects. On the poetry front, we agreed that Bishop was the greatest living American poet, with Lowell, Merrill, Ashbery and Rich not far behind. If someone as knowledgeable as David liked me it seemed there was a faint possibility I might eventually become a writer myself. Also, it seemed that the quality of the poems I was writing had improved.

In January of 1974, *Poetry* magazine, under Daryl Hine's editorship, published some poems of mine, which seemed a big step at the time. Later in the year, Howard Moss accepted a poem for *The New Yorker*. Maybe, just maybe, I was a poet after all. In fact, just two years later, my first book *All Roads at Once* appeared. After that, I never looked back.

Arthur Sze

Revealing and Reveling in Complexity

Interview by Jim Natal

Do you remember the first poem you wrote? What prompted it?

My first semester at M.I.T. I sat in a large calculus class and felt increasingly bored by the lecture. I remember flipping to the back of a spiral notebook, and I started writing phrases to a poem. I was excited at what came to me, and, before the end of class, I had a rough draft. On a subliminal level I realized that, although I was capable at math and science, I didn't want to spend my life in that endeavor. Poetry was a leap into the unknown, and I was prompted to write by an urge to discover something that was truly meaningful to me and not follow family expectation. I wrote that first poem, then a few days later I wrote another poem. Then another. And another. I liked the compression and musicality of poetry. I knew no other form of writing that was so thrilling and compelling.

Was there a teacher, family member, or other person you encountered when you were young who exposed you to poetry?

Instead of a teacher or someone else who introduced me in an exciting way to poetry, I remember, in junior high school, cringing at the way the English teacher approached Coleridge's "The Rime of the Ancient Mariner." She instructed everyone in class to analyze "the albatross" and search for other hidden meanings. So, my first memorable encounter with poetry was tense and negative. In that class, poetry was approached as something that was necessarily difficult, esoteric, and with a correct way to come to terms with its meanings. Later, at a private high school, I had a more sympathetic exposure to poetry. I read poems by Dylan Thomas and Yeats and remember being struck by their rhythms and musicality.

My parents were immigrants from China, and they encouraged me to write only with the understanding that writing well was an important academic and professional skill. Writing creatively was not encouraged at all. My family expectation was that I would pursue something safe and professional: scientist, engineer, doctor, investment banker. Poetry was seen as something wild and risky. Yet, my father had a classical literary education in China that rounded out his career in science in America. I remember looking at and marveling at English translations of Chinese classics in his study—his translations of the *I Ching*, the *Lao-tzu*—so my literary seeds were actually planted there.

Do poets need an MFA (or PhD) for their work to have credibility?

I never attended or graduated from an MFA program, so I clearly don't believe an MFA is requisite to becoming a poet. Nevertheless, I did take two undergraduate poetry workshops that were crucial to my development.

My sophomore year at M.I.T. I took a poetry workshop with Denise Levertov. Denise was the first poet I met, and her passion for poetry was inspiring. She had just taught at the University of California at Berkeley, and I decided to transfer there. At UC Berkeley I took a poetry workshop with Josephine Miles, and she became instrumental to my development. As my faculty advisor and mentor, Josephine enabled me to create an individual major in poetry. I took Chinese language and literature classes and started to translate Tang dynasty poetry into English. To a significant extent, I learned my craft through translation. I was also lucky in that Josephine believed in me. Every two or three weeks I went to her house on a Saturday afternoon and showed her a batch of new poems. She responded to them with great care and insight, and she also directed my reading. At the end of one session, she recommended Rilke, another time Neruda. It was never part of a class or for class credit—these individual sessions with her were precious and foundational to my growth.

Must poets win prizes to be considered established? Are prizes a gauge of success?

It would be disingenuous of me to say that prizes do not matter, because I have received many. Sometimes the cash that comes with a prize has given me precious time to write; sometimes it has given me encouragement; sometimes a prize has brought new readers to my poetry, so I am grateful for what I have received. At the same time, it's important to recognize that writing poems does not depend on that recognition. If I hadn't received any awards, I would still be writing poetry. As Wallace Stevens once wrote, poetry is a source of pleasure, not of honors. It's good to keep in mind Emily Dickinson who wrote and wrote, with little recognition throughout her entire life, and whose courageous body of work is a better measure of success than any prize.

What moves you to poetry? Do you write to be read and published, or for yourself?

I love the intensity and power of language, emotion, and imagination that all come together in poetry. It's an essential language and as necessary as breathing. It helps me live and grow in the world. Writing poems over many years involves growing and deepening and maturing as a complete human being. Solitary as this practice is, I hope that my poetry, like all poetry, speaks to others and is a gift that awakens and moves others to experience the world in profound, essential ways. And I am trying to make my tiny contribution against oblivion.

Science and nature inhabit your work and, even when not the focus or theme of a poem, seem an ever-present low-grade hum in the background. How do you, as a poet, integrate the technical and scientific with the natural and organic?

When I first wrote poems, I tried to avoid scientific vocabulary and structures. I was turning away from M.I.T. and the world of science and turning toward nature. But then I realized that art and science are not antithetical, as some people suppose. As paths of inquiry and understanding, poetry and science can inform and inspire each other. Since I have that scientific knowledge and training, I decided that using it in my poetry was a way to develop rigor and clarity in my writing. I suppose I integrate the technical and scientific with the natural and organic because they balance and enrich each other. Like it or not, we live in a complex, challenging world, and the scientific and the natural are endlessly entangled. I never consciously set out to integrate one with the other; maybe I realized they are already endlessly entwined, and one of my themes or obsessions has to do with revealing and even reveling in that complexity.

How does pan-cultural curiosity and cross-cultural involvement influence your work?

I'd like to quote Theodore Roethke: "I learn by going where I have to go." In the beginning, I translated classical Chinese poetry because I wanted to draw on my ancestry and felt I had so much to learn from those ancient poems. When I graduated from UC Berkeley, I was adventurous and wanted to go somewhere I had never been before. Josephine Miles suggested Santa Fe and gave me the name of a friend, Stanley Noyes. I hitchhiked into town 49 years ago, with only a backpack and my curiosity. I looked up Stan, and he suggested I apply to the New Mexico Poetry-in-the-Schools program. I did, was accepted, and worked for ten years all over the state: on Indian reservations, in Spanish-speaking communities, with incarcerated juvenile offenders, at the New Mexico School for the Deaf (with the support of a sign translator) and in the Penitentiary of New Mexico, where I even worked with an inmate on Death Row. I was excited to discover a part of America I knew nothing about, and I felt an immediate affinity with Native Americans.

When I wasn't working in the schools, for several years I also did construction work as a plasterer—how many contemporary American poets have worked with their hands?—and I learned enough Spanish so that I could read Neruda and Lorca. These steps weren't premeditated, but I wanted to expand my range of experience, and one step led to another. Phil Foss, a poet who taught at the Institute of American Indian Arts, invited me to read my poetry and teach occasional poetry workshops there. I so enjoyed meeting and teaching Native students from tribes across the United States and, eventually, although I did not have a graduate degree, I was hired and became a professor there.

New Mexico is a very multicultural place, and over time, my cross-cultural experiences and connections have deeply informed my poetry. I've used specific Hopi words in my poems, and I've also drawn on a social ceremonial dance at San Ildefonso Pueblo, but these usages have never felt forced. They entered my poems as part of my personal experience. I've always been interested in meeting creative people in other disciplines, and from other cultures. I have always felt I have so much to learn, and my poetry has over time reflected that growth. I don't write a poem thinking about what I can do to make my poetry unique. Instead, if I dig deep and write with openness and risk, I find that the poem I write will emerge and eventually become what it needs to be.

Sheila E. Murphy

Sound. Silence. Privacy. Confidence.

IN MY EARLY LIFE, I was a timid little person everybody liked, sociable, yet self-contained and somewhat lonely. Privacy was both source and protection. I lacked confidence initially. I sought evidence that my early efforts were worthy. Such confirmation would be fuel for harder, more intensive work. Sound was the connective tissue, the signaling of being joined with others in doing things that mattered. The voices of my friends, the importance of being included, the sound of laughter, my own ability to make others laugh.

I learned early that my mind works differently from others, and gradually found ways to navigate their signals while constructing and conveying what was real for me. Recalling what preceded and prompted my poetry stimulates the act of weaving. Poetry is composed of sound and silence, is made in privacy, and builds confidence.

There is no language for first experience. Only feeling. The eyes of my mother, her confident and loving voice, were music. Mother played the piano, sang, and was classically trained on the violin.

The sense of hearing was my first reality. While carrying me, my mother was leading school music programs and continuously playing or performing music. I likely grew accustomed during gestation to sound and may have sensed her positive feeling of creating music. Born premature, I spent my first six weeks in an incubator, keeping my eyes closed, and listening.

At age 10, it was time to select an instrument. Mother and I reviewed a book and decided on the flute for me. Unprompted, I practiced six hours each day, adding to my classical repertoire by routinely playing by ear the music that I liked on the radio by jazz artists and others. My flute teacher, George Opperman, taught music theory so well that when I took theory classes in college, the substance was mere review. Mr. Opperman's vibrato lifted my aspirations for performance, and I relished the muscular purity of his playing, characteristic of the Romantic period. In his one-man factory downtown, he crafted the range of instruments in the flute family, notably bass flutes and alto flutes. To me, there was no more powerful and surprising sound than that of the bass flute, elevating the resonant heft of the instrument far beyond the usual range of the C flute. It was the closest and most confirming version of a foundation for silence, sensing the breath's leading to the meditative tone of "om."

My high school experience was warming and replete with humor and music and literature at the center. In addition to fluting my head off, I sang in small ensemble and madrigal groups under the guidance of Terrence and Patricia Shook, colorful and remarkable musicians immersed in what they were doing.

My classmates and I did skits and filmed them. Good at imitating voices, I performed the role of certain teachers and was applauded for my stand-up work. This built my confidence while adding to the joy of shared experience with people I genuinely liked.

Learning the French language under the tutelage of Sister Miriam Edward, a veritable human beehive, was an electric experience. An American speaker of French, she demonstrated precisely the physical things we needed to do to produce the proper sounds for "r," having us press our tongues against the bottom teeth and then led us in singing wordlessly the tune to "A Bicycle Built for Two." Hilarious. She drew from us a passion for the language. Sound again, the primary inspiration and comfort in my life. At a parent-teacher conference, she told my parents that I had the best pronunciation of French in the class. More confidence. More sound. More confirmation.

The way our teachers spoke about poets appealed to me. It seemed that poets had a license to think, to feel, to be, in ways that transcended what others were afforded. That platform of acceptance appealed to me. Attracted as I was to poetry, these were early days. I was not yet sure how things would work out. I was identified as a flute player. However, I was beginning to suspect that I might be able to create poetry, as I felt the flow of lines that spawned lines of my own.

The urge to write poetry came along full force in my undergraduate years as I read the call for submissions from the literary journal. The quiet of privacy in the evening hours when pen met the page resulted in a charged sense of each poem's coming into being. The act of writing bridged silence and music. It fostered a peaceful confidence. Writing allowed me to perceive what was around me. I needed to allow things to be what they are and to write without the encumbrance of fearing how my message might land. I decided to use multiple pseudonyms for poems I felt needed to be written. I submitted a few under my own name and several more under different names. Most of my submitted poems were published, to the extent that much of the publication was written by me. I held this secret close.

At the University of Michigan during my master's degree program, I discovered yet another dimension of sound. Professor Hamilton, who taught the course in Chaucer, required that we read aloud in Middle English. I spent countless hours in the language lab rehearsing because of my zeal to perfect the sound of *The Canterbury Tales* in Middle English. I loved hearing and speaking the work aloud and was thrilled during one of our extra group sessions to hear Mr. Hamilton favorably acknowledge my vocalizing of that rich and flavorful text. This further heightened my devotion to the intonation of Chaucer in that lovely language.

Poetry is ultimately weaving quiet into music. The fibers of sound, silence, privacy, and confidence, constitute the fabled spinning of straw to gold. So much material, infinite possibilities for making, and the joy of being able to partake in that richness. Ultimately, poetry has become an endless source of abundance, both in what leads to writing and the writing itself. I weave with increasing naturalness now, take risks, and hear both singing and silence as facets of a miraculous music. The pursuit continues, replete with listening, reading, discipline, and relationships that bring surprise. I am grateful for it all, reminding myself each day that I am just getting warmed up.

Burt Kimmelman

My Tutelage

I SUFFER FROM A PECULIAR MALADY. My sense of what a poem is, how it should work, how it might feel—all of this, my understanding of a poem, was determined when I was an adolescent who came into contact with a number of Black Mountain poets. As a working poet, now for more than fifty years, I have been unable to appreciate a poem beyond the framework imparted to me when I was learning what poetry could be.

So, I have viewed my own poetry as an accident—because of my adolescent choice, before I really had any idea what I might do, to attend a college in Cortland, New York where I would come to absorb the writings of Charles Olson, Robert Creeley, Joel Oppenheimer, Paul Blackburn, Denise Levertov, Robert Duncan and others of their ilk. My shortcoming proved to be a strong sense of purpose.

I attended a creative writing workshop run by a Cortland professor, David Toor, in 1965. That same year, I discovered Donald Allen's game-changing anthology, *The New American Poetry 1945-1960*, which had appeared five years earlier. Later I learned that Allen was guided by Olson, former Rector of Black Mountain College, in putting his book together. To create sections of it, Allen devised the post-World War Two avant-garde "schools" readers now know of, which he named *Black Mountain*, *New York School*, *San Francisco Renaissance*, *Beat*, and so on. He also gave Olson's essay, "Projective Verse"—whose influence has been enormous since it first appeared in 1950—pride of place in the Poetics portion of the anthology.

I read Olson with the greatest passion (mesmerized by what I was seeing *on the page*), also Creeley, Oppenheimer, the others—who came to Cortland to lead that workshop. It just so happened that Toor's brother worked alongside Oppenheimer in a Greenwich Village print shop. First Oppenheimer, then everyone else showed up. Blackburn stayed on permanently. Like Creeley and Oppenheimer, he would be a mentor to me.

I was an athlete and wanted to become a football coach, so I enrolled in Cortland's physical education program. Other future writers and artists, oddly, were also enrolled in it—wayward, physically adept students recruited into it, including the future writer and poet Michael (M.G.) Stephens, and Ron Edson who ended up as a painter.

Toor was devoted to us. He gave us a gift greater than we could possibly have imagined. I had fallen in love with Stevens, Emerson, Herbert, Donne, Dickinson. I would come to appreciate these great poets as I read them through the lens of Black Mountain poetics.

Both Stephens and Edson were fixtures in the inaugural writing workshops at the St. Mark's Church-in-the-Bowery Poetry Project (Ron having completed college, Mike having dropped out, as I would). Blackburn had created it. Oppenheimer was its first director. His secretary, then, and its future Director—who would put her indelible stamp on the Project for all time—was Anne Waldman.

Before meeting Toor, I had no knowledge of the Black Mountain poets, any of their forbears such as the Objectivists, or any of their predecessors among the Vorticists and Imagists such as Pound, Williams, and H.D.—the core of American Modernist poetry. Burton Hatlen (who directed the National Poetry Foundation, taking over from the Pound scholar Carroll Terrell) neatly referred to them as "The Philadelphia Three." They all met in or around the University of Pennsylvania in 1905, when still in their teens. (Marianne Moore was just up the road at Bryn Mawr.) These Modernists—as well as Gertrude Stein, Louis Zukofsky, George Oppen et al.—were not to be found in the mainstream collections and were not taught in universities.

The English courses I took—quite other, fundamentally, from Toor's workshop experiences—were steeped in neo-Romanticism and driven by New Criticism. The work to be found in the Allen anthology, however, was fresh, obeying Pound's dictum to "make it new." Allen's book stood as a repudiation of "academic" poetry preceding it. For young poets like myself, this work was far more than enlightening.

Even before I first met Creeley or read his poems, I heard him read a poem as part of a PBS television film. The poem was simply about birds in a tree who were aware of his "presence." The brief lyric ended with a rhetorical question about them there: "And / why not, I thought to / myself, why / not" ("Like They Say," circa 1955). I was stunned by the sense that the poem did not end. Its open architecture was a quality I strove to emulate.

The poem's lack of closure undermined the very edifice of the neo-Romantic poem that depended on a sense of crisis or a revelation leading to a closure, "the sense of an ending" in the words of the great critic Frank Kermode. Such a formula could not accommodate the explorations of a Creeley or, before him, Williams (think of "The Red Wheelbarrow" or "This Is Just to Say"). I would discover an even more open-ended quality in Blackburn's poems.

Poetry's mainstream was facing a challenge, one that, even in the mid-sixties, I had yet to comprehend as that. The poets of nostalgia were being represented in a particularly well-known anthology, *New Poets of England and America*, which appeared just before, and then, in a new edition, just after the appearance of Allen's book. The poets they selected were celebrated and canonized. Their anthology contained work written by not a single poet included in *The New American Poetry*, and vice versa—this "other" anthology, virtually forgotten now, most often taught from in the universities, then.

The college-assigned collection lacked the focus within the avant garde upon language in and of itself (what Creeley called "the thingness of language"). That sense of *words* was coalescing in me, starting in my college days. Then, after leaving college to live in the East Village, I attended a workshop led by Oppenheimer. That sense of words, and of the freedom from formalism's constraints, deepened. There's another thing about my Black Mountain legacy. While the poetics grew out of the teaching, writing, and thinking that took place at Black Mountain College, in rural North Carolina—and while participants in that grand conversation arrived there from various points on the globe, many of them rural—a direct outgrowth of the college was a jolt of energy and innovation that dramatically affected arts communities in a number of cities, San Francisco and New York especially. (The story of Basil and Martha King's migration from Black Mountain, first to San Francisco, then to Manhattan and ultimately Brooklyn, is iconic.)

That the New York School was already helping to establish its namesake city as the center of the art world, well before Black Mountain closed its doors, does not fully account for the breadth and vibrancy of art activity in New York, along with poetry and other disciplines, linking back to the college. As for poetry—the post-war avant-garde especially indebted to Black Mountain—new *forms* of poetry, which were alien to the mainstream and radically different, would come to the fore in vibrant urban centers.

In large measure because of emigration to New York from Black Mountain, its poets (also Blackburn and a young Amiri Baraka, then LeRoi Jones) contributed significantly to a downtown literary scene. This community was made up of the likes of Frank O'Hara, Allen Ginsberg and, along with Oppenheimer, younger people, such as Diane di Prima, who was later to be viewed as a hybrid (according to Donald Allen's categorizations, that is—some writers, like William Bronk, did not fit neatly into the various schools). Perhaps no more vivid sign of this community, which we might now view as disparate, is the fact that Ginsberg's long poem *Howl* was first typewritten by Creeley.

Out of this downtown New York City scene, eventually the Poetry Project birthed its own poetic practices, which sponsored later New York School (Ted Berrigan, Bernadette Mayer, Ron Padgett, Lewis Warsh, et al.), later Beat (di Prima, Waldman), and then *L=A=N=G=U=A=G=E* poetry (Charles Bernstein, Bruce Andrews, et al.). In common among these new schools' proclivities, was the *urban lyric*.

The benchmark of this "urban" poem was the 1967 publication of Blackburn's *The Cities*. The poems in his collection were first disseminated in little magazines of the fifties and sixties. Arguably, it was Blackburn's Black Mountain poetics, holding imagery to be crucial (in keeping with the precepts of Pound, H.D., and Williams), which gave rise to various evocations of the cityscape. What the Black Mountain impulse contributed to this new poem of the city was the precise image, including on the page, along with a candid voice.

Both can be found in the work of O'Hara (one of the poets comprising the original New York School). Yet the sense of written language as material existence, in and of itself, as can be found in Black Mountain and, earlier, Objectivist poetry and poetics, could manifest through a voice embodying the breakdown of statement. Particles of speech stood on their own (as in, vividly, Blackburn's poems, before his George Oppen's).

A poet like Oppenheimer contributed to this emerging complex with a palpably urban grit (perhaps coming through subliminally in his juxtapositions). The very feel of the city was critical in his poems. Here is the title work of his 1962 book, *The Love Bit*:

the colors we depend on are
red for raspberry jam, white
of the inside thigh, purple as
in deep, the blue of moods, green
cucumbers (cars), yellow stripes down
the pants, orange suns on ill-
omened days, and black as the
dirt in my fingernails.
also, brown, in the night,
appearing at its best when
the eyes turn inward, seeking
seeking [. . .].

An explanation of how the younger di Prima was working, having absorbed this aesthetics, and for a time working closely with Jones
/ Baraka, is encapsulated by remarks she'd make much later about this
period (in an interview with Waldman): "All my writing was completely
predicated on getting the slang of N.Y. in the period in the early 50's, down
on paper somehow or another." Here is one of her late-fifties lyrics from
her first collection *This Kind of Bird Flies Backward*:

In case you put me down I put you down
already, doll
I know the games you play.
In case you put me down I got it figured
how there are better mouths than yours
more swinging bodies
wilder scenes than this.
In case you put me down it won't help much.

Communal living and jazz make up di Prima's language here. The poem
also proclaims the sense of being free within an alternative way of living. All of this is embodied in her word "swinging." There is melody in
di Prima's verse lines that, echoing both agreements and disagreements
the poem's speaker encounters through daily happenstance, espouses the
democratic.

One final aspect of Black Mountain poetics should be mentioned. There
was, not in any obvious way, a philosophical aspect in the poetry of some-

one like Creeley, so too as regards Olson's or Duncan's poems. But it was Creeley who put together something for me, which I had been observing in North American avant-garde poetry although I was failing to see a bigger picture. These poets, along with Oppen and Bronk (and Stevens, who had also appeared in Cid Corman's journal *Origin*, and the *Black Mountain Review* edited by Creeley), grasped the phenomenological implications of quantum mechanics (evident in some of their work).

Through Oppen's sister, June Degnan, then publisher of the *San Francisco Review*, Bronk appeared on the national landscape in 1964 when his collection *The World, the Worldless*, whose manuscript had been edited by Oppen, was brought out by New Directions. Especially of interest, here, is the fact that Bronk had been the last poet to be cut from the Allen anthology, ostensibly due to space issues.

Yet Olson's stunning blurb on the back cover said a lot about what Black Mountain poetics was: "I may have, for the first time in my life, imagined a further succinct life." (Bronk had once shown up at Black Mountain, wanting to visit Olson, and was met by Duncan who told him that Olson was asleep and could not be disturbed. Olson then tried to visit Bronk at his home in Hudson Falls, New York, but Bronk was traveling with his sister in Europe. The blurb originates on a postcard Olson penned to Bronk, expressing regret at having missed him. The published correspondence between the two poets is fascinating.)

Olson's comment—the "further succinct life"—riveted me as a young poet, who was steeped in both Olson's and Bronk's writings. (I first met Bronk in Cortland, in 1966, and we began exchanging letters and sometimes poems.) Olson's work was, in many ways, quite distant from Bronk's—yet not in some fundamental way that, as it happened, extended beyond Pound's notion of "condensare" (his coinage) while comprehending that. In some respects, just as Oppen's work differed from Bronk's on the surface, while, nevertheless, their respective writings shared a vision (as is professed in their correspondence), that vision was partaken of by Creeley and others. Olson and Bronk entertained a fundamental world view.

The word *world* possessed a special heft for them (also for Creeley, Stevens, Oppen and others—today, in poems by Michael Heller and Hugh Seidman, for example). They also shared a certain understanding, and appreciation, of language that fit with a common cosmology. Creeley was pivotal in this intellectual as well as artistic history (for years, Olson famously carried on an intense dialogue with him—note the fat volumes of their published letters).

I'll always cherish what, for me, was an epiphanic moment, when I opened a letter from Creeley, which contained his permission to quote passages of his work in my then-upcoming critical book on Bronk. Creeley had scribbled an encouraging note on the permissions page itself, in the margin. His inscription included an apostrophe in quotes, and with the exclamation mark to be found in a line from a poem of Bronk's: "World, world!" The phrase comes from Bronk's fifties poem "In Contempt of Worldliness," which, initially, he sent to Olson in a letter that continued a conversation they'd been having about Oppen. The phrase would later appear in Bronk's 1964 book:

> How one comes
> to despise all worldliness! World, world!
> We cling like animal young to the flanks of the world
> to show our belonging; but to be at ease here
> in mastery, were to make too light of the world
> as if it were less than it is: the unmasterable.

Creeley's imitation *cri de coeur*, in the margin of his response to my entreaty, could well have come from the title of Oppen's poem "World, World—" that concludes his 1965 collection *This In Which* (note the title's privileging of pronouns). I mean to suggest, all the same, a bidirectional influence here (as might be seen in letters between Bronk and Oppen), in addition taking into account another poem of Bronk's, "The Arts and Death: A Fugue for Sidney Cox," which appeared in his 1956 volume *Light and Dark*, hence preceding Oppen's poem. Therein Bronk writes: "World, world, I am scared / and waver in awe [. . .]."

Creeley's inscription confirmed for me what I was already intuiting about our avant-garde poetry. That was something not being comprehended by the poets in the post-War "academic" scene. It was something essential within the Black Mountain experience. Creeley was signaling me, making sure I got it all. The poem below is indebted to him. I have come to realize how much, over the years, he was supportive of my work (of course my debt to Bronk, Olson, Oppen and others is not new news):

The World at Dawn

I wanted so ably
to reassure you . . .
. . . and got up, and went to the window,
pushed back, as you asked me to,
the curtain, to see
the outline of the trees
in the night outside.

—Robert Creeley, from *The World*

Lying still
on my bed,
I look through

my window.
Outside, trees
stand into

the sky, their
branches and
leaves above

roofs, chimneys.
The dawn is
white. I am

looking out
on the world.
There is its

light. A car
goes by not
far away.

I might say
something like,
if I were

dying, "I
will leave this
world." The word

world is so
important
for poets—

some knew it
was a word.
Stevens, Bronk

and Oppen,
Creeley are
all gone. They

thought about
words. They knew
how very

desperate
words are. Their
words are mine.

Dennis Barone

Eileen R.
Tabios

Rafael Jesús
González

Tony Trigilio

Stephanie
Strickland

Susan Terris

EDITOR

Julie Marie
Wade

Eileen R. Tabios

My First Book

I WAS FIVE YEARS OLD when I created my first book.

Or so my mother says in an essay discovered among her papers two years after she passed in 2012. I'll start there. Here's Mama:

My daughter, Eileen Tabios, was five years old when she wrote her first book. I have been smiling over this memory recently as our family celebrates the publication of her first two books: a poetry collection, *Beyond Life Sentences* (Anvil, 1998), and a group of essays and interviews about Asian American poets, *Black Lightning* (Asian American Writers Workshop, 1998).

I still remember how, as a little girl, Eileen visited me in my bedroom one day and pointed to a red box where I kept pens, paper clips and pencils. "I need a box for my books—that'll do," she announced.

"I've been keeping my books in this," she explained as she held up an envelope bulging with little folded papers, "but it won't close and I don't want to lose them."

She put the envelope on my desk. "I'll show you the last book I made," she offered, taking one of the folded papers and unfolding it. Her "book" was a strip of paper cut from her brother's school supplies. I imagined her little hands cutting the paper with sharp scissors and felt alarm. I was about to say something about being careful with scissors, but she proceeded to "read" her book to me.

"The grass in the park is wet," she said, pointing to the bottom of the first space of the folded paper. I saw a green smudge.

"See the little raindrops," she said, pointing to penciled dots. "But I was not wet because Manang* Rosing held the umbrella over me."

"This is Trixie," Eileen said as she touched a little horizontal stick figure that had a circle on one end and a line that curved downward on the opposite end. I noticed that she depicted her puppy's legs with two little lines below the horizontal line.

"And this is me," she said as she pointed towards a stick figure beside Trixie.

"This is Manang Rosing. She's holding an umbrella so I won't get wet," she continued as she touched the taller stick figure beside her. One arm was connected to a short line that, in turn, was connected to a half circle above the shorter figure. I made a mental note to tell the housekeeper not to take the child out for a walk when it was raining.

"We watched some boys marching around in the park," Eileen continued, touching another space on the folded paper. I saw a row of stick figures. Each figure had one arm raised and extended forward. The row of figures managed somehow to look like marching soldiers. Then it dawned on me that she must have seen the students who were in the ROTC (Reserve Officers Training Corp.) of the local college. They usually had weekly drills in the park near our house.

"This old man was angry with the boys," my daughter added, touching a tall stick figure who stood slightly apart from the row, "because he kept yelling at them."

"The rain did not stop so Manang Rosing said we should go home before we got soaked like the boys," my little writer went on.

"Then, we are home," she said as she touched the last space on her book. "This is you," she touched the shorter of the two figures, "and this is Daddy," she touched the taller one.

"What's this?" I asked, touching a red smudge at the end of my husband's arm.

"That's the bag of cookies that Daddy brings home," she replied.

"And what's this?" I touched one of two squares which I thought were boxes.

"That's the church next door. Don't you know? And this is our house," she added, touching the other square. She sounded like I should know our neighborhood better.

"My daughter, the writer," I thought fondly. Then more hopefully, I thought to myself, "Why not?"

"Can I have the box now, Mama?" she reminded me as she folded her "book" and placed it in the envelope. After I emptied the box, she took it from me and proceeded back towards her room. I heard a "Thank you" before she closed the door.

I sat down on a chair as I mused, "My daughter, the writer." I was delighted by her early leaning towards scholarly pursuits. I was impressed with the originality she showed in making her books. "My daughter cuts paper books, not paper dolls!"

Then I thought, "I should teach my little writer some words that she can use when she talks about her books. Words like "paperback" for her book, "library" for her box, and "page" for the spaces of the folded paper. I could teach her to number the pages of her book with one short line for page 1, two short lines for page 2 and so on. This also could help her understand the concept of numbers since she already could count from one to ten on her fingers.

I began to become more excited as I fantasized further. There would be my little writer talking to our friends in the living room. She would be "reading" one of her books, and the guests would be under her spell. She would finish her book and fold it. Then she would hold up the folded paper and ask no one in particular, "Do you know that my book is called a paperback?" And she would answer her own question, "It's because it does not have a hard cover."

"And I have my own library," she would continue, holding up her red box for all to see. "My Daddy and Mama have their library, too," she would add, pointing to the tall bookshelves against the wall of our living room.

I laughed quietly, imagining the looks on our friends' faces. I thought some would look incredulous and others impressed. They would ask, "Where did this little girl, this baby, get her ideas? What five-year-old says paperback or library as easily as she says ice cream or candy?"

"My little writer," I would answer proudly, looking fondly at my daughter who would be returning to her room, oblivious to the surprise she would have caused.

As I ended my fantasy, I noticed my husband had arrived and was standing in front of me with a quizzical look.

"You're laughing all by yourself. That's not a good sign. What's so funny?" he asked.

"Your daughter has a surprise for you," I replied. "Did you remember to drop by the bakery for something?"

"What were you laughing about?" my husband persisted as he sat down. "I brought home some doughnuts. They're still warm."

"I'll let your daughter tell you her surprise. I'm glad you remembered to bring home something to eat. It seems she expects that of you whenever you come home," I said, rising to tell Eileen of the doughnuts.

—END OF MAMA'S TALE—

* * *

Years later, I would stumble across my mother's recollection of my first book. Intriguingly, for another project I had created a visual poem that sought to reproduce what I held in my memory as "My First Book." It was a different book than what my mother described. What I remembered creating as my first book—and I thought I created it as a two or three-year-old—was an untitled piece of asemic writing that unfolded on three pages from a folded strip of paper.

The first page featured a green Crayola scrawl at the bottom of the page. The green scrawl, to me, presented the thought of "The grass is green."

The second page featured a yellow Crayola circle on top of the page. The yellow circle, to me, presented the thought of "The sun is out shining."

The third page was like the first page except that the Crayola scrawl was brown, not green. The brown scrawl, to me, presented the thought of "The sun burnt the grass."

I know—so young, and already I had a dark side! (That darkness is certainly evident in my first U.S. poetry collection, *Reproductions of the Empty Flagpole*, published by Marsh Hawk Press in 2002.)

In comparing my mother's recollection with mine, I note how the book I recall is simpler than the one my mother remembered in her essay. Thus, I believe my memory contains the first—or at least an earlier—book rather than the one described in my mother's essay. I must have created several such books, based on her recollection that I had shown her "an envelope bulging with little folded papers." Either way, what she and I both remember is that I was creating books long before I could read or write.

I will always be grateful to my mother for cherishing and encouraging my early impetuses to create books. As I write this essay, my books as a writer and editor number nearly a hundred from publishers in 10 countries and cyberspace. Whether or not I explicitly state so in the books' acknowledgements, I dedicate each and every one to my beloved mother. She had helped me to become a writer by enthusiastically loving me into becoming a writer. *Agyamanac unay, Mama.*

---

* *"Manang" is a Filipino honorific expressed before the name of an older person.*

Dennis Barone

These Hills, This Mountain-Laurel

I.

During my senior year in college, I wrote a long-poem called *The House of Land*. Once upon a time the poet finished his career with the long-poem or commenced one in mid-career, but I decided to begin with one. I think at Bard College I wrote over one-hundred pages, but during the following years I rewrote and shortened the work. Wallace Stevens wrote Paule Vidal on June 18, 1952: "Usually, at my age a poet starts to write a long poem chiefly because he persuades himself that it is necessary to have a long poem among his works." Of course, Stevens must have been facetious here for he had already composed many of the greatest long poems of the century. In 1986, my first year in Connecticut, Spectacular Diseases of Peterborough, England published my long poem with a thoughtful introduction by the novelist and poet Toby Olson. For years I thought or I recalled that I lifted lines—just a couple—out of Stevens's "The Comedian as the Letter C" and used them in my poem. In the winter of 2014 out of curiosity, I went back and looked for these lines. It took me a few moments. For they are not from "The Comedian," but from "Notes Toward a Supreme Fiction." On page 19 of my poem, I wrote:

> Unless I know the ground
> upon which my feet are to stand
> I can say nothing of the sky.
> These hills, this mountain-
> laurel in black clay, this
> patter of the white-tail,
> these apples.
> We haven't seen when we thought we saw.
> Summer exiles from the Chapel of Holy Innocents.

I probably just quoted more than I needed to, but I wanted to get to that chapel name which I have always loved. That really is the name of the Bard College Chapel. We may not have been either as holy or as innocent as we should have been.

And in Part II of "Notes Toward a Supreme Fiction,"—It Must Change, section five, one reads:

> Long after the planter's death. A few lines remained,
> Where his house had fallen, three scraggy trees weighted
> with garbled green. These were the planter's turquoise
> And his orange blotches, these were his zero green,
> A green baked greener in the greenest sun.
> These were his beaches, his sea-myrtles in
> White sand, his patter of the long sea-slushes.

So, I didn't exactly quote from Stevens, but just repeated a bit of the rhythm of the lines. And I like the fact that Stevens mentions here a "planter's death" and what "remained" because in my poem I refer frequently to a historical figure named Yahley—a name I thought neat partly because it could so easily be confused with Yahweh (God)—whose ruins in the Ramapos of New Jersey I would hike by as a teenager and yes there were some "scraggy trees" as well as the remains of a foundation. Stevens, too, as a young man hiked in these hills though more often a bit south of my often-trod paths. "The foundation lies buried beneath the skin," I wrote in my long-poem. So, I had here an actual place ground as well as a poetic ground on which to stand or to leave.

2.

I had excellent teachers of English and History in high school. One history teacher once invited three politicians to speak to us. Senator Hightower speaking for the Republicans had the most political clout but I found him somewhat dull as did my classmates. Jim Bouton, the former Yankee pitcher, spoke on behalf of the Democrats. For me, he seemed too frivolous a voice though the crowd loved him. The third speaker, Jarvis Tyner, a vice-presidential candidate for the United States of America spoke on behalf of the Communist Party. After the speakers finished, some of us went up on the stage to ask questions. Most students went to Bouton, some to Hightower, and one to Tyner. I thought he had wisest words; the sharpest mind. After that day I bought a subscription to the *Daily World*.

Perhaps at that time a file began somewhere in Washington D.C. with my name on it. But I threw the Feds a curveball by signing up for some student group to support the re-election of the President. For several decades I saved the issue of the *Daily World* that proclaimed "Nixon Resigns—Was Deal Made?"

What does this have to do with poetry? Three things: the relationship of the disciplines of history and poetry has been a constant concern for me; a playful contrariness has characterized my art and my scholarship; and soon after this high school political assembly and discussion my first poems were published.

I think the first one appeared in the *Daily World*. It concerned a northern New Jersey group of people abused, discriminated against, and exploited for centuries. But I can't be sure. My first poems might have been published in Charles Plymell's *Cold Spring Journal* or Maureen Owen's *Telephone*. In both, if I recall correctly, I had a concrete or visual poem and a short lyric inspired by another poet: Walt Whitman and Terry Stokes.

I gave up on the accentuated visual aspects of the poem, but stuck with the wide-ranging reading and the short lyric or philosophical musing. While in college I added two other broad sorts of poems to the lyric—the notebook poem and the project poem—and these categories continue to the present. My most recent work has a project poem called "Day by Day" and my 2012 book *Parallel Lines* contains a notebook poem, "Scarf." For a project work certain rules are established at the start and a length of time at least for a gathering of words and lines. A notebook poem simply organizes idea and phrases from a notebook, sort of man with a notebook (instead of with a movie camera).

3.

Sometimes I worried that the historian and artist must be kept separate. When I began teaching I told colleagues I would not teach creative writing, as if teaching it would cheapen it in some way. I began an early essay published in *Boundary* 2 perhaps in 1980 with this claim: "The poem is primary. All theory secondary." I may still believe that—though not so rigidly and yes I did teach creative writing for more than thirty-years. I took sustenance in a simple phrase. Susan Howe once told me—many years ago—to refer to her as a poet-scholar. I also like the title of Denise Levertov's book of essays: *Poet in the World.*

I did not ever see myself as a social activist poet but always a poet active in the world. During college I started a literary magazine, *Tamarisk* (along with Debbie Ducoff; later we became husband and wife). During graduate school, along with Eli Goldblatt and Gil Ott, I hosted some Philadelphia poetry readings. In Hartford I've hosted readings but also written a host of commentaries for the newspaper on affordable housing, immigration, as well as the poets of Connecticut from the Revolution to the present.

4.

I think rather than fret about the anxiety of influence I have embraced influence. It is interesting to note that tribute poems depend to a large extent on knowledge of the subject and therefore the audience for such poems must be limited (though what poem except perhaps a Presidential inauguration poem does not have a limited audience?).

"Time will stand still for a few weeks as the weather itself stands still in August before it removes to Charleston, where it will stand still a little longer before it removes to some place in South America like Cartagena, which is, I suppose, its permanent abode—the place where all the catbirds go, not to speak of the other birds which live in our garden for a while"—from a letter by Wallace Stevens.

Stevens wrote that letter at home in Hartford (July 27, 1949). You might have heard that in 2014 the Episcopal Church put the house at 118 Westerly Terrace up for sale. There was a realtor's open house and many of us went that day to see the house once more, now empty of the Rev. Pendleton's family's furniture. The emptiness gave a different sense of the house and this emptiness we paired with greetings to friends. How can friendship be known and expressed outside of language? You'll recall that a first offer for the house came from a group who thought they might change the residence into a historic house museum of sorts—an ambitious, courageous, and perhaps foolish plan, one conceived much too quickly and under the pressure of possibly losing the opportunity, the deal. Well, it did fall through and the house remains in private hands—perhaps as it should or so *The Hartford Courant* editorialized at the time. Once Jim Finnegan and I went to see the belongings of Stevens that are warehoused elsewhere in Connecticut. His bed was remarkably small, "penitent" as I say in a poem, small, especially for such a large fellow.

"The bed of old Wallace Stevens is less than you'd imagine . . ."—so, I begin my poem "House for Sale" (published in the *Wallace Stevens Journal* in 2015 and in my book *Second Thoughts*, 2017, page 6), a tribute poem. And another such poem, a Stevens's tribute poem, "An Ordinary Evening," (the *Wallace Stevens Journal* 2007; the *Visiting Wallace* anthology, pages 7-8; and in my book *Parallel Lines*, 2011, pages 24-25) recalls the poet as an elderly man and ends with poet "recalling / The hikes he took last spring." And so what inspires us in our early twenties, may stay with us and continue to do so in our mid-sixties.

> The house is not built,
> not even begun.
> This house is a cloud,
> this bliss of stars,
> a princox of evening:
>
> June evening, a green
> evening sighted as if
> young and without any
> scent or shade. This
> house half-dissolved in
> evening.

Rafael Jesús González

The Gasp

I WAS BORN INTO FLOR Y CANTO, in xochitl in cuicatl, flower & song, poetry taught me by my father Jesús and my mother Carmen (who before she married compiled a collection of poems, in Spanish of course, meticulously typed on two-hundred-fifty pages bound in an embossed binder from the custom house in Cd. Juárez where my aunt Luz worked, the first book I ever attempted to illustrate, to my mother's consternation, at the age of three or four.) They had me learn poems I barely understood (of Yanko, a boy who yearned for a violin, and of a blind man who begged from them who could see) for me to recite at family gatherings every Sunday at my Papanito Diego's and Abuelita Chayito's house. I remember once my tía Conchita burst into tears at a "poem" of my own that I recited.

I did not know what made my aunt cry, but I had some notion of the power of words. I did not just learn simply by rote the poems I recited nor did I say them without feeling them. I had my childish understanding of Yanco's yearning to make music and of the pain of the blind beggar. I imagined with horror utter darkness, of not being able to see the sunset or the moon, the trees, the flowers, the play of light upon the mountain, the faces of the ones I loved.

And so I grew my poet's heart in love with language, I do not know if because it allowed expression of my amazed perceptions or if it was language itself that shaped them. I have often wondered. I speak of language because it is inseparable from poetry, but the root of flor y canto, flower & song goes much more deeply. What I was taught (before and simultaneously with language) was love. And a keen sense of beauty. (Without these I doubt there would be flor y canto at all; without the flower, would song be possible or worth hearing?)

I loved the shape and color of things (drawing and painting was my first passion, poetry of a different sort, a related world.) The Earth was the source of my wonder, driving with my family at dawn through the desert covered in lavender desert verbena or on vacation in Ruidoso helping my grandmother look for white violets under the ferns by the noisy stream (for which the place was named), the shapes of stones, the flight of birds.

Spanish, of course, was my first tongue and when I began to learn English at the age of seven at Lamar Public School, I acquired another tongue, another world. It was not easy at first. If we spoke Spanish at school, we would be punished. One morning, my mother walked me to school and then went on with my little brother, Arturo, to my grandparent's house a few blocks away. I entered a deserted playground; I was terrified. (The teacher had announced a day of vacation, but I had not understood.) I walked back home to an empty house and sat on the porch, lonely, afraid, confused, till my mother returned with my grandmother and I was smothered in kisses and hugs. I failed first grade.

When I was in the fourth grade, the principal recommended that my father enroll me and my brother, Arturo (two years younger than me), at Bailey school for "retarded" children. So my father took us. We could not have spent more than half an hour and the principal said that we did not belong there and recommended that we change schools. My parents went into debt and bought their first (and only) house in another district so that my brother and I could attend Morehead Public School. Whatever problems there were disappeared.

And all along I wrote, in Spanish and in English into which I grew. My teachers often said that my writing was "poetic," but my poems were private, to be shared only with my father and mother, my grandmother Chayito in cards I made for their birthdays, saint's days, and other occasions such as Valentine's Day (a thing I do for very special people in my life even now.)

These are the happenings of my formative years. Happenings are the food of poetry, but it is from one's inner life that poems are made. I was shy, introverted, clumsy at sports, repelled by competition. I was religious, an altar-boy at St. Patrick Cathedral, worried that my mother and father did not think regular attendance at mass was particularly important. I prayed to God, a vague, stern "father," and I had a notion of the holy but it was not the same as my experience of the sacred which I've always had. Holiness was somehow polite, although awing, abstract; sacredness was wild, alive, little to do with good or bad; it was a gasp in the heart.

It was what I felt accompanying my father on his business trips to little towns in Texas and New Mexico when I gazed at the infinite horizon, the mountains that changed shape according to the light, the white desert poppies. At church, it was the colored light streaming through the windows that had little to do with the scenes from the tragic life of the young rebel rabbi that they depicted and whose name was given me (because it was also my father's.). It had to do with beauty that I found in nature and in art, but a beauty that had little to do with pretty; it could be terrible as in a storm at sea and the Gran Coatlicue, the black paintings of Goya. It had much to do with joy, but not necessarily so; it had also to do with the darknesses that cut joy. It was the catch in the heart. It has no words; it is the task of poetry to give words to the wordless.

Sacredness had to do with aesthetics at the root of its meaning, perception, an alerting of the senses that fires the heart. It was the difference between a Safeway market in El Paso with its vegetables and fruit arranged in neat straight rows under stage-lights, with little smell, hardly any talk between costumers and clerks, and the Mercado in Juárez with its stands of vegetables and fruit stacked in pyramids or piles, a tumult of colors and smells, its stands of piñatas and sarapes and folk-art, a carnival of color and form, lively interchanges between buyers and sellers. The senses were alive. On the road trips my father took us to Mexico, each village and town had its own smell and art form: Saltillo its sarapes, Celaya its cajeta, Tonalá its pottery. We were taken to wonders: the pyramids of Teotihuacan and the rococo church of Santa Prisca in Taxco. In Mexico city we stayed in an old hotel with an imposing patio across from the Alameda Central park not far from the elegant Hotel del Prado where my parents took us to see Diego Rivera's Sueño, and to the museum in the old Casa de la Moneda just off the Zócalo to see the Stone of the Sun, and to the museum in Chapultepec where I was introduced to the two disquieting Fridas with their open hearts.

My final year of grade school was difficult; my shyness intensified painfully and I developed a stutter that made it difficult for me to utter a simple sentence and worried my parents so that they sent me to speech and psychotherapists. Graduating, I went to El Paso High School and there I regained my tongue with the help of my speech teacher enough that I became involved in school politics and in my junior year was elected President of the Student Council. My acquaintance with poetry let me excel in my English classes. There I read Thoreau which led to my first act of civil disobedience when, as Student Council President of the host high school of the Southern Association of Student Councils Convention, I refused to sign letters of refusal to applications from the segregated Black schools. I would not be budged. The letters were signed by the Secretary of the Association. I learned justice from my father and mother, an extension of the love they taught which had much to do with my decision to study medicine.

My parents could not afford to send me to college; on graduating, I joined the Navy in order to obtain the benefits of the G.I. Bill and served in the Hospital Corps, two years at Corona Naval Hospital in Norco, California, two with the 1st Marine Brigade at Kaneohe Bay, Territory of Hawai'i. It was an intense time during which I learned a great deal, read a great deal, wrote much, and confirmed my aversion to the military.

At the end of my discharge, I enrolled in pre-med at Texas Western College of the University of Texas (later the University of Texas at El Paso) on the G.I. Bill. It was then that I began to "go public" with my poems (many that I wrote while in the navy.) I completed all my required courses for pre-med, but it was English and Spanish literature that grabbed me. Two papers that I had written in my English courses, one on the pre-Hispanic literature of Mexico and another on Beat Literature, were published in literary magazines. One poem, titled "Apathy," from my stint with the Marine Corps, submitted for an anthology of the National Student Poets Association received the 3rd Place Award. (It was the only poetry competition that I have ever entered.) A poem that I wrote in my freshman year from an experience working after class in my father's store in el Segundo barrio became one of my most anthologized poems and put me in the vanguard of Chicano literature:

Come, mother—
    your rebozo trails a black web
    and your hem catches on your heels,
you lean the burden of your years
on shaky cane, and palsied hand pushes
    sweat-grimed pennies on the counter.
Can you still see, old woman,
the darting color-trailed needle of your trade?
    The flowers you embroider
    with three-for-a-dime threads

cannot fade as quickly as the leaves of time.
        What things do you remember?
Your mouth seems to be forever tasting
the residue of nectar hearted years.
Where are the sons you bore?
        Do they speak only English now
        and say they're Spanish?
One day I know you will not come
and ask for me to pick
the colors you can no longer see.
        I know I'll wait in vain
for your toothless benediction.
        I'll look into the dusty street
        made cool by pigeons' wings
until a dirty child will nudge me and say:
        "Señor, how mach ees thees?"

I took part in poetry readings and folk began to call me "poet." I could
say that I had always written (lived) poetry and, though it was part of me,
I never called myself a poet; it was the exalted title of those masters I had
memorized as a child and read as an adult.

In my senior year, I became a born-again pagan and when it came time
to graduate, to the disappointment of my family, I decided that medicine
was not my calling. I decided to teach instead. After spending the third
year of my National Education Act Fellowship traveling in Europe, teaching in universities during the Viet-Nam war which I actively opposed
organizing Teach-ins and counseling conscientious objectors, I realized
the truth of my decision: it was for that gasp, that catch, those serendipitous revelations of pedagogy that defined education for me.

Outside the long lawns roll
the honey sunlight on their green tongues
& in the class-room I mouth the brittle truths
I've love-shopped & paid for with forked coin.
        (I sat one February day
        in the white sanctuary of Delphi
        trying to break the almond
        from its tough & furry husk—

Apollo never came
& I caught cold.)

My students stare
& wonder what I've tried to say
        of logic
                or love
                        or just plain words
        like fuck.
I do not know myself
                sometimes.

But then one day I say some thing I do
        not know I say
                (while thinking of
                Casals' tender wrestling with Bach
                Barcelona's Ramblas by moonlight
                the clams' love-life on Cape Cod
                        or Viet-Nam)
& suddenly
one boy shatters his sulk—
some dirty city star
        long ago swallowed by his sight,
        surprised by awareness, shoots,
        tear-washed & sharpened
        from his eyes.

This gasp, this catch in the heart (what I think a poet friend called the jaguar in her heart) is what I look for in the marvels of the Earth, in art, in poetry, in life. It is why I raise my voice against that which diminishes life, that sins against the gasp; it is the root of my activism. When in 1983 I took a leave of absence from my teaching at Laney Community College in Oakland, California to organize the International Day of Nuclear Disarmament and undertake direct actions of civil disobedience, I found myself in Lompoc Federal Prison for attempting to block the test of the MX Missile at Vandenberg Airforce Base, I knew that I was there for life and on a scrap of paper with the stub of a pencil smuggled in, wrote:

I am here—
I wear the old-ones' jade—
it's life, they said & precious;
turquoise I've sought to hone my visions;
& coral to cultivate the heart;
mother of pearl for purity.

I have put on what power I could
to tell you there are mountains
where the stones sleep—
hawks nest there
& lichens older than the ice is cold.

The sea is vast & deep
keeping secrets
darker than the rocks are hard.

I am here to tell you
the Earth is made of things
so much themselves
they make the angels kneel.
We walk among them
& they are certain as the rain is wet
& they are fragile as the pine is tall.

    We, too, belong to them;
they count upon our singing,
the footfalls of our dance,
our children's shouts, their laughter.

I am here for the unfinished song,
the uncompleted dance,
the healing,
the dreadful fakes of love.
    I am here for life
        & I will not go away.

I can say that I have always written poetry but I never considered it for a profession. I wrote poems though it took me a long while to own to the title of poet that other folk gave me. I became a teacher of literature and Creative Writing though I never took a course in Creative Writing myself. I have always worked my art in solitude never having been part of a writers' group, perhaps an advantage I have foregone. It is shyness perhaps, perhaps a privacy that my muses (two, one with a Spanish tongue, the other with an English one) have wanted to preserve. I have not published much. When students asked about publishing, I told them that publishing does not a poet make. If they sent a poem to a friend for a birthday, or to the family for a holy day, they were publishing. I mostly publish by sharing my poems with family, friends, colleagues through an e-mail list that has grown with the years. It is my way of keeping in touch, sharing where I am in my thoughts, my concerns, to remind them of the season's turn, alert them when the moon is full.

The writing of poetry is always an act of becoming, and when at the over-ripe age of eighty-two, I was named the first Poet Laureate of Berkeley, beloved city I have called my home for nearly half a century, I was stamped as such. And when I go away, as we all must inevitably do, and my remains (at the desire of my family) are returned to El Paso del Norte, border of my disbelief, to be buried in the desert of my birth, one side of the granite headstone will read:

Si la vida es
luciérnaga en la noche
que su luz breve que sea
sea brillante.

and the other:

If life is
a firefly in the night
let its light however brief
be bright.

Tony Trigilio

Passing Through Our Brief Moment in Time:

A Poetics of the Ordinary

ON SEPTEMBER 19, 1961, around 10:30 in the evening, Betty and Barney Hill were driving in the White Mountains, near Lancaster, New Hampshire, when they noticed a bright light in the sky that seemed to be following them. The light grew larger and brighter. Barney pulled the car over and stepped out to investigate with his binoculars.

Their lives would never be the same after that night. Three years later, under hypnosis, the Hills described the strange light as an extraterrestrial aircraft. The two claimed they had been captured by aliens who brought them into their ship and performed medical experiments on them before returning them to their car in a deliberately induced fugue.

The Hills' experience is the subject of my most recent book, *Proof Something Happened*, a collection of documentary poems published in spring 2021 by Marsh Hawk Press. I realize this is an unusual way to start an autobiographical essay on my development as a writer. But I begin here because *Proof Something Happened* can serve as a metaphor for how my writing life has been shaped by the relationship among poetry, narrative, and the uncanny.

No ready vocabulary exists to describe the experience of encountering a literally out-of-this-world "other." The Hills could not prove to a skeptical public that something actually happened to them in the White Mountains. Our sense-based, utilitarian language is inadequate to describe such a happening, whether what occurred was an actual alien abduction or an intergalactic mirage.

Words define the boundary between the real and unreal, which would be a perfect arrangement if our lives unfolded exclusively within the limits of what we already know. But what happens when you come face-to-face with something that is beyond words because it is, as the Hills claimed, literally from another world? How do you describe what we have no language for?

Poetic language is the only kind of discourse that helps me untangle what is strange, weird, and sublime in my everyday lived experience. Poetry forces me to pay attention. It requires me to slow down my emotional and intellectual attention spans and actually listen to what the unknown world is telling me. But I also write from deep anxiety that some part of my environment might go un-represented unless shaped into language.

The relationship between anxiety and speech was an inescapable part of my childhood. I was fortunate to grow up in a household and extended family where a couple different languages were spoken—English and Italian. I was exposed at any early age to all the ways language can fail to convey anything.

What's more, my mother suffered from a severe hearing disorder, a malady that runs in our entire family, and we all took for granted that no matter how earnestly we try to communicate, our words inevitably leave gaps in understanding.

I could've been intimidated by the confusing childhood realization that the words I used were simultaneously trustworthy and fickle. Instead, each effort to try to represent a feeling, idea, or experience in language became something of a dare. I took it personally.

As much as we distrusted language in my family, we just as fervently believed in it. We didn't need to read Wallace Stevens to know that words are "necessary fictions."

Language is our ticket into community, and in my family, narrative was what kept us thriving. As a child, I was riveted by the colloquial oral histories my mother and father told over dinner—stories of how their first-generation immigrant families navigated the bizarre ways of this new country and how their otherness frustrated them. They pined for what they portrayed as our inevitable return to Italy, "the old country," as they called it.

My impulse for narrative comes from my family's stories. But poetic narrative encompasses more than just plot-based storytelling that builds toward cleanly structured epiphanies. Poetic narrative is cross-cut with associational, often interfering images and phrases, and by counterpoint rhythms and voicings that interrupt the trajectory of the standard narrative arc. This dance between narrative linearity and flash-cut interruption is what makes the most opaque or elusive experiences speakable.

* * *

I've been fascinated for as long as I can remember by language that tries to describe uncanny experiences, like that of the Hills, without explaining them away. Like many poets, my first experience with this kind of discourse occurred in sacred texts, where the representation of extra-sensory phenomena depends on the figurative language of poetry. Consider Ezekiel: the more you try to describe the flaming chariot you see in the sky, its wheel rims full of eyes, the stranger and more unfamiliar—and more poetic—your language becomes.

My first secular poetry obsession was Dylan Thomas, whose work taught me that poems express what can't be contained by the limited logic of everyday language. Like the religious texts of my Catholic childhood, Thomas's work induced a feeling of vertigo that, paradoxically, also helped me see the world more clearly—that encouraged me to pay attention to the ineffable landscapes beneath the surface of things. I couldn't take vision for granted anymore. Seeing was a matter of urgency.

"Begotten, not made, one in Being with the Father," we recited from the Nicene Creed each week in Catholic mass, describing the mystery of the incarnation—a line that I couldn't stop saying out loud when I was younger, even though it bewildered me to no end. Its regular rhythm clashed with its sinewy semantics, which only heightened the difficulty of imagining the god-made-flesh we were celebrating in church every Sunday. Eventually, I decided that this line from the Nicene Creed was the only appropriate verse to follow the opening lines of Thomas's "*Altarwise by Owl-Light*," one of the favorite poems of my youth (possibly because it was absolutely inscrutable to me): "*Altarwise by owl-light in the half-way house / The gentleman lay graveward with his furies / Begotten, not made, one in Being with the Father.*"

I was thrilled by my earliest exposure to religious texts, in the Bible and in the tidy, liturgical missalettes of weekly church service. But poetry was special primarily because it was *secular*. Thomas's difficult, mystical poems weren't trying to persuade me to be a good Catholic, which would've been a futile effort, anyway. I converted to Buddhism a quarter-century ago, a religion with its own tradition of voicing what seems beyond language (but without the metaphysical doom and gloom of original sin).

* * *

Music was the bridge between religious language and poetry for me. All thanks for this goes to my sister, Mary Ann, whose Beatles records affected me profoundly from the moment I first encountered them at age six. The lyrics in songs like "Eleanor Rigby" and "Nowhere Man," especially, offered a vocabulary to describe the solitary nature of being human, a difficult feeling I was just starting to experience at that age, and one that I barely understood.

These songs suggested, as religious texts did, that a luminosity can be found inside those intensified moments of feeling when we are alone with ourselves. They taught me something about solitude and writing that would become clearer many years later when I first read Allen Ginsberg's "Improvisation in Beijing," from his collection *Cosmopolitan Greetings*.

"I write poetry," Ginsberg says, "because I want to be alone and want to talk to people."

Still, to develop as a poet most of us need the guidance of others, especially in the United States, a country that undervalues art in general and dismisses poetry in particular. I grew up in a middling, utilitarian, rustbelt city, Erie, Pennsylvania. It was not the kind of place where you could find many artistic role models. I was grateful for those rare moments when an adult asked me what I was writing and actually wanted to hear my answer. The first to do this was my fourth-grade writing teacher, Ms. Omark.

She convinced me that I could write autobiographical material that other people might want to read. I composed my first serious poem in 1974, age eight, an anxiety-ridden response to my abject fear of tornadoes. We didn't have a basement at home. I wrote about my terror that we had nowhere to hide if a tornado touched down in our neighborhood. Ms. Omark liked the poem so much that she asked me to rewrite it on poster board, and then she taped it to the front of her desk.

Later, in my first undergraduate poetry workshop at Kent State University, I began to take poetry seriously as an artistic practice. We had very little space in our family to cultivate the arts. But here I was, in a college-level classroom with twelve other students who wanted to write poetry. Our instructor, Mac Hassler, guided us with formal and informal writing prompts, and he also taught us how to keep a regular journal and then to incorporate our journaling into finished poems that could have an individual shape and voice all their own. This pedagogy is a foundation for the creative writing courses I teach now at Columbia College Chicago. Back then, it was a revelation that the four walls of the classroom could be an environment for intimate life-writing.

Poetry, then, came to me foremost as a personal thing: an art form that documents our emotions as they collide with the outside world. Poetry revealed itself as the artistic practice best suited for documenting the mysterious emotional narrative arc of my life.

Poems give me access to the vulnerable, the strange, the unsayable in what otherwise seems quotidian. Whether I'm writing documentary or autobiographical poems, I'm drawn to material that dramatizes ordinary, everyday moments in time that evade the rudimentary language of social exchange.

* * *

A poem is a document of an ordinary person passing through a brief moment in time. This spirit is at the core of a documentary collection like *Proof Something Happened*, and it's also crucial to my autobiographical work. In an immediate, ongoing way, this aesthetic serves as the conceptual blueprint for my multivolume experiment in poetic memoir, *The Complete* Dark Shadows *(of My Childhood)*, published by BlazeVOX [books].

As part of my research for this series, I'm re-watching every episode of the old 1960s–1970s gothic soap opera, *Dark Shadows*, which I saw every afternoon with my mother when I was a small child. Back then, sitting in front of the television with her on the sagging, gray couch in our living room, I became obsessed with the show's main character, a two-centuries-old vampire named Barnabas Collins. I was afflicted with constant nightmares about him, and I went so far as to hunch my shoulders at night, thinking this would prevent him from biting my neck when I slept. (Evidently, it worked: when I checked the mirror every morning, I was relieved to find no vampire puncture wounds.)

I write one sentence in response to each *Dark Shadows* episode, then shape these sentences into a poetry / prose hybrid form, using each sentence as a trigger for autobiographical explorations. The most recent book, *Ghosts of the Upper Floor*, the third installment in the series, was published in 2019 by BlazeVOX. The show ran for 1,225 episodes, which means I'll need several more volumes to finish the project. Proust had his madeleine; I have my vampire.

Proof Something Happened also recovers a lost moment in time in order to document its emotional history. I'm not just referring to the four hours of missing time the Hills experienced during their alleged abduction. The book also recalls the subsequent years when these two ordinary people tried to prove—in the cold war's repressive culture of containment—that something truly did happen to them that night in 1961.

The Hills' most ardent skeptics mocked their experience. They received hate mail, much of it racist. Theirs was an interracial relationship at the very beginning of the civil rights movement, and the hostility toward what they claimed happened in 1961 was heightened dramatically by white supremacy. The trauma of trying to explain their alleged abduction to a skeptical public was exceeded by the racial trauma inflicted upon them by that same public.

Letters arrived constantly from people who alleged to have seen UFOs, many of whom claimed that they, too, had come face-to-face with extraterrestrials. Some of their correspondence also was pure crankery from the fervently religious. "Enclosed is a book which will enlighten you in regard to Spiritualism," one such letter begins, "and which, we hope, will cause you to have nothing to do with the 'Prince of the Power of the Air' (the title the Bible gives to the Devil)."

This was not just a sci-fi captivity narrative, nor was it only a critique of the postwar politics of race. As I became immersed in the research and writing, I realized I was also writing a love story. Two individuals, deeply attached to each other, suffering a terrifying aloneness because of an experience most people dismissed out of hand.

Two ordinary people passing through their brief moment in time together.

"I feel a love of the ordinary to the point of revolution," Bernadette Mayer writes in *Piece of Cake*, a collaboration with then-husband Lewis Warsh that documents in autobiographical prose the day-to-day particulars of one month in their lives, August 1976.

Forty-five years later, her words are just as relevant. It's difficult, but necessary, to pay attention close enough to make art that documents an ordinary life—whether I'm rendering my life or that of a person in a docu-poetry collection—especially in a culture whose power structures actively discourage such attentiveness.

The effort to see clearly, to cast one's vision both wide and deep, requires deliberate, conscious effort in a moment in time like ours, dominated by marketing language that translates our subjective experiences into con-stellations of data points, a moment in time saturated with artificial needs and ersatz satisfactions. We have to find our own counter-discourses for this process of pacification. Ever since childhood, I've turned to poetry to imagine a language for vision. I want to read and write poems that teach me to see. "The eye altering," as William Blake writes, "alters all."

Stephanie Strickland

Late to the Party

MY FATHER, an electrical and mechanical engineer, a designer, a builder, a plumber, a sound engineer, a sailor—and later, a CEO—stayed home during my WWII childhood because he was inventing things the war effort thought it needed. He built his own automobile—this was Detroit, it was not uncommon. His father did the same and was also a hunter and all-around outdoorsman. Consequently, it has never occurred to me that a thing could *not* be done, if sufficient respect were paid to *the laws of nature*, as my father would have called them.

His knowledge was primarily perceptual, sensing the depth of water by the color, navigating by feel. I was mystified by what he saw in the air— these *laws of nature*—for indeed he just *saw* how things worked, the way I might see a marigold. And he was frustrated, and I was frustrated, that I could not do the same. He acquired, but disdained, book knowledge that supported his intuition, and he never trusted books nor any "pencil-pushers," lawyers, ad men, or other nefarious workers in language.

This is a complicated heritage for a child who feels drawn to write. A disavowed, if not proscribed activity.

We moved to Chicago; I adored the huge buildings. My father bought architecture books with pictures, including one of Frank Lloyd Wright's Fallingwater, a house built over a waterfall. By fifth grade I wanted to be an architect and was drawing plans, I loved math. In some respects, I have become an architect, an envisioner of digital- or installation- or, indeed, print-poem-structures. These I do see in the air, somehow, and work to make them materially or virtually real.

My Scots-Irish grandmother believed in fairies. These could almost be spied in the thick lilies of the valley growing beside her driveway, or skirting the Queen Anne's lace that we would stop the car to inspect in a field. She married a German doctor during World War I and was harassed by the local authorities: was she hoarding food in her attic? Her husband had been exiled by his mine-owning family in Silesia for helping to organize mine workers there. (My poem "slippingglimpse" in *Zone : Zero* uses language from a Silesian folk tale, "The Passion of the Flax.") In this country he went from mining to medicine and died, of blood poisoning contracted during a surgery he was performing, when my mother was only 18 months old, before antibiotics. There was a great unspoken emptiness at the center of their lives, my mother's and my grandmother's.

My Welsh-English grandmother's attic was the third floor of a house. It was full of rooms and trunks and old books, including journals from the 19th century that were bound as books. She wanted to capture me, perhaps from my mother, certainly from my other grandmother—I lived near them both. This contest was perhaps the first of many tugs-of-war where I felt pulled apart in very different directions. She was strict and formal and taught me card games. She made superb pies, using cherries from the tree in her garden. She kept icy cold water in ribbed glass refrigerator bottles. Hummingbirds came to her window.

My active, archivist grandmothers! The one who believed in fairies had been a suffragist (suffragette, she would have said) and a musician, earning her widowed way as an accompanist. The other, the archivist of journals, the Christian Scientist, a woman who had gone to teach on Indian reservations, who had studied to be an opera singer, then stayed home, imperially, but not happily.

My mother? The center: so quiet. Not thinking she should speak. Not believing she had anything worthy to say. She could serve. She could clean. She could help. She could listen and she did, to neighbors and to strangers. She was sought out. She did not seek. She did not speak.

This is a complicated heritage for a child who wants to write. *Especially* . . . because I knew, unspoken, that she *wanted* me to write. *For* her, it seemed, to my young self. And that made it hardest of all. Hard to know whether it was *I* who wanted to write. If I were to do so, beyond kindergarten crayoned copying of verses, I felt and feared I would never escape her orbit of silence and service, the unbuilt and the unsaid. I wanted the life of the easily-traveling-about men, the easily-speaking men.

I tasted words, I loved poems. My fairy-acquainted grandmother had taught me songs and rhymes. That is, she taught me formal structures. So, on all sides, formal structures—musical or architectural or engineering— all mesmerizing, immersive, enchanting: structures that encode the laws of their making and their meaning.

Nonetheless, all the way through college, I solved only math and science problems and wrote only critical essays about literature and history. Even before it ended, I had a child and two more within five years, more physically constrained than I had felt even my mother to be. At home with babies in the 1960s, my creative resource was the radio and the explosion of popular music in that decade. Inspired by Jimi Hendrix and others, yet half against my will, reluctantly, wrenchingly, I began to scratch words on scraps of paper—and to throw them away. This situation changed only when my youngest son was almost two years old. I vividly recall rocking him in a room lit only by flashes from Christmas tree lights bursting against the ceiling. Overhearing my brother and a friend speaking softly, I heard this friend mention his poems. It suddenly, truly *suddenly*, struck me—dawned on me: he doesn't tear them up. And that was it! There was tearing up—and *not* tearing up.

I have raised children, worked as a college librarian, and cared for several family members with long-term disabling illnesses, which I continue to do. The library job allowed me to get both an MS and an MFA in exchange for my work hours. I was originally rejected from the college's MFA program. They told me that I could write prose, but not poetry, and suggested I take a summer workshop with Cynthia Macdonald. I did and was then admitted to the first year of a new graduate program at Sarah Lawrence. It was able to draw on the college's outstanding undergraduate writing resources: teachers Jane Cooper, Grace Paley, Galway Kinnell, June Jordan, Alexis DeVeaux, and many others. Adrienne Rich and Muriel Rukeyser visited. The library had collected contemporary poetry since 1926.

Only late in my life have I taught writing and digital literature. In the course of my library work in the 1980s, I faced the challenges of automating a college library and digital search. In my poems, I speak in the vicinity of science, one might say, including computational science, which I believe to be a juggernaut of the 21st century. I speak in forms—not only inherited literary forms, but forms the world is rich in. I focus on what women know and their varying historical experiences. I have been interested in the body, the sensing intuiting body of the engineer, the body of the nursing caretaking mother, the body of the woman who knows—and knows that she knows, even though the world does not affirm her knowledge. I have not ever wanted to claim one knowledge at the expense of another.

My 2019 book, *How the Universe Is Made: Poems New & Selected* (Ahsahta), has a through-line focus on women and forms of embodied knowledge. *Ringing the Changes* (Counterpath Press, 2020) is created from code that draws on the ancient art of tower-bell ringing. For sport, ordinary folk in 17th-century England rang every possible arrangement on seven bells. Sounded from a church tower, changes are resonant peals, but in this book they are samples of language taken from writers who explore intertwined real / virtual worlds. A much smaller interactive toy companion, *Liberty Ring!*, probes Liberty through passages sampled from many writers, including *The Framers*. In both works, seven threads of thought weave new contexts for each other, in a ring, or in a line, as forms of civil conversation.

My mother died when I was 40. Simone Weil is the mentor of my adult life. I found her writings serendipitously and immersed myself in them in my thirties and after my mother's death. Weil is a philosopher and a mystic, initiated in many forms of knowing and unknowing, interested in ethics, but interested most in a kind of spiritual knowing that is not possible in language alone. She was also awkward and difficult and exasperating, trying to do things in a world not at all ready to hear what, or how, she had to say. All of my books, after the first, have been affected by Weil and my relationship to her. She speaks in Bell 5 of *Ringing the Changes*.

I am late to the party because so many changes are needed before some of us can start.

Julie Marie Wade

Small Doors

SINCE I FIRST BEGAN WRITING as a child, a small door inside my head has been propped open, perpetually. In the beginning, I didn't know it was there, but now I'm sure I couldn't close it, even if I tried—that essential parenthesis—that necessary gap between the frame and the wall where the first light and the last light stream through.

Everywhere I go, everything I read or watch or listen to—which is another way of saying everything I *learn*—I'm collecting. (Perhaps it's hoarding? Perhaps this is a symptom of my time?) I might want to teach that text or refer to it in class. I might want to place it in my own work as a touchstone, something to linger on or pivot from, something akin to a key.

I think about this door in my head as though it were a real door leading to a real room, which is what the word *stanza* means after all, in Italian—a *room* or *stopping place*—somewhere to linger.

Sometimes I think about the house where I grew up, how we had many doors that didn't close or more precisely, many doors I never saw shut. The door to my bedroom couldn't be closed all the way because my mother put a shoe rack there the week I turned thirteen. She said this was a better way to store my shoes than the boxes in my closet or underneath my bed, but I never completely believed her.

When my parents said they didn't want "closed doors" in their house, I knew they weren't just talking about real doors, with hinges and knobs and push-button locks. The doors they spoke of were symbols, representing something else. They thought if they could walk down the hall and peer into every room, their view unobstructed, nobody could be keeping secrets. That nobody was me.

Even if I was just trying to get dressed, pulling on my pants or tights under a bathrobe, struggling to slip a shirt over my head before pulling off a towel—*how I got so hot and sweaty every time!* Secrecy and privacy are easy to confuse, I realize, but most of our lives seemed hidden in plain sight, especially mine.

((((((

When I think of a door propped open, I picture the word *ajar* and then the two words that sound just like it: *a jar*. (Hear it: a tiny breath. See it: a small caesura.) One describes the state of being partially exposed or not all the way closed while the other is a container, usually made of glass and sometimes shaped like a bell, which reminds me of the brilliance and sadness of Sylvia Plath.

When I think of a door propped open, I also think of a door jamb, which may help to prop it open in the first place, and how I love the homophones *jam* (which might be made at home and stored in jars, the way my mother made and stored it for many years) and *jamb*, with the silent "b" I always felt that I could hear my own sixth sense for stealthy letters. They never snuck up on me.

And when I think of *jamb* spelled this way, I also think about *enjamb*, the opposite of end-stopped or door-closed; of words spilling over inside the stanza-room, refusing to be jammed, refusing to be jarred, or otherwise contained completely.

But to enjamb a line also means to break it, and so I think of the jar broken, the glass glittering at the threshold of the partially open door, and how I must be very careful not to sweep it under the rug, as my parents would prefer, but to collect the pieces—which, when referring to glass, are most often described as *shards*—a lovely word which contains *hard* because they are—those beautiful, impossible fragments.

Every day of my writing life, which is also my teaching life, which is also my life as a daughter and a partner—those two, against each other, painfully spliced, the filial and the queer—I am always at some point down on my hands and knees with a dustpan and a tiny broom, sorting that small caesura. I am trying to collect the shards, which I may use for something—a *mosaic*, let's say—because I have learned that sifting through the fragments of the broken jar is the only key to keep this room unlocked, the only jamb to keep this door unclosed, the only prop to hold this parenthesis, in perpetuity—and sometimes, if I'm very lucky, in perspicacity, too—*open*.

((((((

In the house where I grew up, there was a half-door in the middle of the hallway, a little rectangle cut into the wall. It had a different kind of knob than all our other doors—it looked like a button but pulled like a lever—and inside that partial room (*semi-stanza?*) my mother kept (*hoarded?*) all the candles she had ever bought. We never burned them. I don't know why. But when there was a sale, she couldn't resist coming home with candles, stacking them many rows deep—long white tapers, small white votives, and the fat round kind that were pink or peach or green as pine needles. Their wicks were always white, though—proof they had not been lit.

Sometimes, when we brought the fresh laundry upstairs, instead of piling our sheets and pillowcases inside the linen closet, my mother would open the half-door and stuff everything inside, including my favorite quilt. "If we leave these here for a few days, they'll smell like the candles," she promised—which they did! I learned then that fragrances could become their own kind of lyrics, harmonizing the fruity and floral, the tangy and spicy, and nothing in my childhood ever smelled as good as a blanket that had been sent to time-out in that little half-room in the hall.

Sometimes, I think of pulling the clean sheets out of the candle-stanza with my mother, breathing them in before I spread them out on my bed. Memory is also a door, you see. *Cracked* can be a synonym for *ajar*. Less open, but still open. Slightly. Now, again, and perhaps always, I must leave the door of memory cracked.

Sometimes, when I conjure that room in my head, I see candles everywhere, bright as a field of flowers, every one ablaze.

I think of Plutarch: *The mind is not a vessel to be filled but a fire to be kindled.*

I think of Yeats: *Education is not the filling of a pail but the lighting of a fire.*

I think of the way we build upon each other, in writing, in teaching, all our minds at work. In loving, too. In loving, maybe most of all.

Biographies

Dennis Barone, as author or editor, has published twenty-six books including the prose work *Second Thoughts* (Bordighera Press), the volume of poetry *Parallel Lines* (Shearsman Books), and the anthology *Garnet Poems: An Anthology of Connecticut Poetry Since 1776* (Wesleyan University Press). He retired from the University of Saint Joseph in 2020 after thirty-four years of teaching. He is currently Poetry Editor for the Wallace Stevens Journal.

Philip F. Clark is the author of *The Carnival of Affection* [Sibling Rivalry Press, 2017]. He currently teaches at City College, New York, where he received his M.F.A. in Creative Writing in 2017. The Poetry Editor of *A&U Magazine*, his work has been published in *Tampa Review*, *The Marsh Hawk Press*, *Tiferet Journal*, *Lambda Literary*, and *Vox Populi*, among other publications. His poetry website is *The Poet's Grin*: https://philipfclark.wordpress.com/

Alfred Corn has published eleven books of poems, two novels and three collections of essays. He received the Guggenheim fellowship, an award from the Academy of Arts and Letters, and one from the Academy of American Poets. He taught Creative Writing at Columbia, Yale and UCLA. More information at: https://en.wikipedia.org/wiki/Alfred_Corn

Denise Duhamel's most recent book of poetry is *Second Story* (Pittsburgh, 2021). Her other titles include *Scald*; *Blowout*; *Ka-Ching!*; *Two and Two*; *Queen for a Day: Selected and New Poems*; *The Star-Spangled Banner*; and *Kinky*. A recipient of fellowships from the Guggenheim Foundation and the National Endowment for the Arts, Duhamel is a distinguished professor in the MFA program at Florida International University in Miami.

Rafael Jesús González taught Creative Writing & Literature at Laney College, Oakland, California where he founded the Mexican & Latin American Studies Dept. Four times nominated for a Pushcart Prize, he was honored by the National Council of Teachers of English for his writing 2003. He received a César Chávez Lifetime Achievement Award 2013 and one from the City of

Berkeley 2015. In 2017 he was named Berkeley's first Poet Laureate. http://rjgonzalez.blogspot.com/

Jane Hirshfield's ninth poetry collection is *Ledger* (Knopf, 2020). She's also the author of two now-classic books of essays, *Nine Gates & Ten Windows*. Honors include fellowships from the Guggenheim and Rockefeller foundations, Academy of American Poets, and NEA, and her work appears in *The New Yorker*, *The Atlantic*, *NY Review of Books*, *TLS*, *Poetry*, and ten editions of *The Best American Poems*. A former chancellor of the Academy of American Poets, she was elected in 2019 into the American Academy of Arts & Sciences.

Burt Kimmelman has published ten collections of poems as well as nine volumes of criticism and over a hundred articles mostly on literature, some on art, architecture and culture. His latest book is *Visible at Dusk* (Dos Madres Press, 2021), a selection of his essays. Forthcoming is *Parapet: New Poems* (Marsh Hawk Press, 2022). More about him is available at BurtKimmelman.com.

Basil King, born in London, England in 1935, has been painting for over seven decades and writing since 1985. He does both in Brooklyn where he has lived since 1969. He has published ten books and a dozen chapbooks of poetry and made thousands of art works. *Basil King: MIRAGE*, a film by Nicole Peyrafitte and Miles Joris-Peyrafitte features his art and text. www.basilking-marthaking.com

David Lehman is the author of *One Hundred Autobiographies: A Memoir* (Cornell University Press) and *The Morning Line* (Pittsburgh), his most recent collection of poems. He is the founding and series editor of *The Best American Poetry*. He also edited *The Oxford Book of American Poetry*. His book on noir, *The Mysterious Romance of Murder*, is forthcoming in spring 2022.

Phillip Lopate is the author of over fifteen books (poetry, fiction, nonfiction) and is most known for his essays "Bachelorhood", "Against Joie de Vivre", "Portrait of My Body" and his anthology *Art of the Personal Essay*. He is a professor in the Columbia graduate writing program, and lives in Brooklyn.

Denise Low, Kansas Poet Laureate 2007-09, is winner of a Red Mountain Press Award for *Shadow Light*. Other recent publications are a memoir, *The Turtle's Beating Heart: One Family's Story of Lenape Survival* (University of Nebraska Press; *Wing* (Red Mountain); *Casino Bestiary* (Spartan); and *Jackalope* (Red Mountain, fiction). She teaches for Baker University's School of

Professional and Graduate Studies. She lives in California's Sonoma County, homeland of Pomo people. www.deniselow.net

Mary Mackey, *New York Times* best-selling author, became a poet by running high fevers, tramping through tropical jungles, being caught in volcanic eruptions, swarmed by army ants, threatened by poisonous snakes, and reading. She is the author of 14 novels and 8 collections of poetry including *The Jaguars That Prowl Our Dreams*, winner of the 2019 Eric Hoffer Award for the best book published by a small press. https:marymackey.com

Jason McCall holds an MFA from the University of Miami. His collections include *Silver*; *I Can Explain*; *Dear Hero,*; *Mother, Less Child*; *Two-Face God*; *A Man Ain't Nothin'*; and *What Shot Did You Ever Take* (co-authored with Brian Oliu). He and P.J. Williams are the editors of *It Was Written: Poetry Inspired by Hip-Hop*. He is a native of Montgomery, Alabama, and he teaches at the University of North Alabama.

Sandy McIntosh is publisher of Marsh Hawk Press. His recent memoirs, *A Hole in the Ocean: A Hamptons' Apprenticeship* and *Lesser Lights: More Tales from a Hamptons' Apprenticeship* feature stories of the writers and artists of Long Island's Hamptons who were his mentors. He has published fifteen collections of poetry and prose as well as three award-winning computer software programs. His filmscript won the Silver Medal in the Film Festival of the Americas.

Indigo Moor is Poet Laureate Emeritus of Sacramento. His fourth book of poetry, *Everybody's Jonesin' for Something*, took second place in the University of Nebraska Press' Backwater Prize. *Through the Stonecutter's Window*, won Northwestern University Press's *Cave Canem* prize. His books, *Tap-Root* and *In the Room of Thirsts & Hungers*, were both parts of Main Street Rag's Editor's Select Poetry Series. Indigo is on the visiting faculty for Dominican's MFA program.

Sheila E. Murphy's recent books: *Golden Milk* (Luna Bisonte Prods); *As If to Tempt the Diatonic Marvel from the Ivory* (Broken Sleep); *Reporting Live from You Know Where* (Meritage, i.e.,and xPress(ed), winner: Hay(na)ku Book Award. She's the author of 44 books of poetry and multiple chapbooks. Her book *Letters to Unfinished J.* won the Gertrude Stein Award (Green Integer Press). Her work has appeared in *Poetry*, *Hanging Loose*, and *Passages North*. https://en.wikipedia.org/wiki/Sheila_Murphy.

Jim Natal is the author of three books of lyric poems: *Memory and Rain*, *Talking Back to the Rocks*, and *In the Bee Trees*, as well as two collections written in contemporary haibun form—*52 Views: The Haibun Variations* and *Spare Room*. A multi-year Pushcart Prize nominee, literary presenter, and co-founder of indie publishing house Conflux Press, his work has appeared in many journals and anthologies. For *Chapter One*, he interviewed Arthur Sze.

Gail Newman, former SF Coordinator for CalPoets and educator at the SF Contemporary Jewish Museum, edited *Room, a Women's Literary Journal* and two anthologies of children's poems: *C is for California* and *Dear Earth*. Publications include *Nimrod International, Prairie Schooner, Ghosts of the Holocaust* and *The Bellingham Review. Blood Memory*, her second collection, chosen by Marge Piercy for the Marsh Hawk Press Poetry Prize, won the 2020 NCPA Gold Award for Poetry. www.gailnewmanpoet.com

Geoffrey O'Brien is the author of nine collections of poetry, most recently *The Blue Hill* (Marsh Hawk Press Poetry Prize, 2018) and *Who Goes There* (Dos Madres Press, 2020). His eleven prose books encompassing memoir and cultural history include *Dream Time: Chapters from the Sixties, The Phantom Empire, The Browser's Ecstasy, Sonata for Jukebox*, and *Where Did Poetry Come From: Some Early Encounters*. He lives in Brooklyn.

Kim Shuck is a poet, educator, and troublemaker from San Francisco. Shuck is the solo author of eight books of poetry and prose. She is editor, assistant editor or co-editor of ten collections of poetry. Her awards include a PEN Oakland Censorship award, a Northern California Book Award for being a groundbreaker, and an American Academy of Poets National Laureate Fellowship. Kim's latest book is *Exile Heart* from That Painted Horse Press.

Stephanie Strickland's ten books of poetry include *How the Universe Is Made: Poems New & Selected* (2019) and *Ringing the Changes* (2020), a code-generated project for print based on the ancient art of tower bell-ringing. Other books include *Dragon Logic, True North*, and *The Red Virgin: A Poem of Simone Weil*. She has also published 12 collaborative digital poems, most recently *Liberty Ring!* (2020). www.stephaniestrickland.com

Arthur Sze is a poet, translator, and editor. His eleventh book of poetry is *The Glass Constellation: New and Collected Poems* (Copper Canyon, 2021). Previous books include *Sight Lines*, which won the 2019 National Book Award for Poetry, *Compass Rose*, and *The Ginkgo Light*. He has also published *The Silk*

Dragon: Translations from the Chinese. A professor emeritus at the Institute of American Indian Arts, he lives in Santa Fe.

Eileen R. Tabios has released over 60 collections of poetry, fiction, essays, and experimental biographies from publishers in 10 countries and cyberspace. In 2021, she released her first novel *DoveLion: A Fairy Tale for Our Times.* Her award-winning body of work includes invention of the hay(na)ku, a 21st century diasporic poetic form, and the MDR Poetry Generator that can create poems totaling theoretical infinity. More information is at http://eileenrtabios.com

Susan Terris (Editor) is a freelance editor and the author of 7 books of poetry, 17 chapbooks, 3 artist's books, and 2 plays. Journals include *Air/Light, The Southern Review, Georgia Review, Prairie Schooner, Blackbird,* and *Ploughshares.* She has had poems published both in *Pushcart Prize* and in *Best American Poetry.* Her most recent book Dream Fragments won the Swan Scythe Press Award. www.susanterris.com

Lynne Thompson is the 2021-22 Los Angeles Poet Laureate. The author of three books of poetry, Thompson's work has appeared in *Ploughshares, New England Review, Colorado Review, Pleiades,* and *Best American Poetry,* among others. Her latest poetry collection, *Fretwork,* was selected by Jane Hirshfield for the Marsh Hawk Poetry Prize. She sits on the Boards of Directors of Cave Canem and Los Angeles Review of Books.

Tony Trigilio's recent books of poetry are *Proof Something Happened* (Marsh Hawk), *Ghosts of the Upper Floor* (BlazeVOX), and *White Noise* (Apostrophe). His selected poems, *Fuera del Taller del Cosmos,* was published in Guatemala by Editorial Poe (translated by Bony Hernández). He co-edits the poetry journal *Court Green,* and is a Professor of English and Creative Writing at Columbia College Chicago. www.starve.org

Julie Marie Wade is the author of 13 collections of poetry, prose, and hybrid forms, most recently *Skirted: Poems* and *Just an Ordinary Woman Breathing.* With Denise Duhamel, she authored *The Unrhymables: Collaborations in Prose,* and with Brenda Miller, *Telephone: Essays in Two Voices.* Wade teaches in the creative writing program at Florida International University and makes her home in Dania Beach with Angie Griffin and their two cats.

New Titles in the Chapter One Series
From Marsh Hawk Press

Creativity: Where Poems Begin
BY MARY MACKEY

A meditation on how the sources of creativity emerged from a vast, wordless reality and became available to a poet. As such, it is not only a memoir; it is an exploration of the power and process of becoming a poet. What is creativity? Where do creative ideas come from? What happens at the exact moment a creative impulse is suddenly transformed into something that can be expressed in words? To describe creativity is extraordinarily difficult because the moment of creation comes from a place where language does not exist and where the categories that determine what we see, hear, taste, and feel are not immediately present. In our daily lives we tend to live on the surface, unaware of the complexity and richness of what lies below. Poetry creates itself, bubbling up from the depths until it reaches that part of our brains that transforms consciousness into words. Poetry chooses the poet. The poet did not choose it. This book is a journey to that place where all poems begin

Plan B: A Poet's Survivors Manual
BY SANDY McINTOSH

University teaching positions have often been the preferred destinations of young American poets. But with the success of MFA programs, when tens of thousands of graduates vie for the limited availability of part-time and full-time teaching posts, many will have to look elsewhere for work. Many will have to devise and follow a Plan B. The award-winning poet, Sandy McIntosh, having lost an early teaching assignment, launched a life-long career in projects that utilized his writing abilities. Instead of corrupting his poetry, he shows how working in different writing genres enhances personal creative work, at the same time it provides a financial basis upon which to continue building one's craft.

Craft: A Memoir
BY TONY TRIGILIO

An exploration of the writer's craft through a series of short, linked personal essays. Each chapter features an anecdote from the author's development as a writer that illustrates craft elements central to his body of work. *Craft: A Memoir* is an effort to understand craft through discussions of the direct experience of writing itself—through stories of how Trigilio became a writer. When we talk about "craft" as writers, we frequently focus on clinical, literary-dictionary terms such as language, narrative, structure, image, tone, and voice, among others. To be sure, this book considers such conventional craft elements—especially questions of language, narrative, and structure—but as a book focused on storytelling and memoir, it also emphasizes craft elements such as: generative strategies and revision; persona and voicing; appropriation and remixing; documentary poetics; traditional and experimental poetic forms (including the role that an expanded conception of "ekphrasis" can play for twenty-first century writers); the relationship between music composition and poetry; the role of narrative in lyric poetry; the importance of the ordinary and the mundane; the importance for poets of reading prose; and the artistic benefit of blurring the boundary between history and craft.

Where Did Poetry Come From: Some Early Encounters
BY GEOFFREY O'BRIEN

A memoir in episodes of some early encounters—with the spoken word, the written word, the sung word—in childhood and adolescence, encounters that suggested different aspects of the mysterious and shapeshifting phenomenon imperfectly represented by the abstract noun "poetry." From nursery rhymes and television theme songs, show tunes and advertising jingles, Classic Comics and Bible verses, to first meetings with the poetry of Stevenson, Poe, Coleridge, Ginsberg, and others, it tracks not final assessments but a description of the unexpected revelations that began to convey how poetry "made its presence known before it had been given a name."

Titles From Marsh Hawk Press